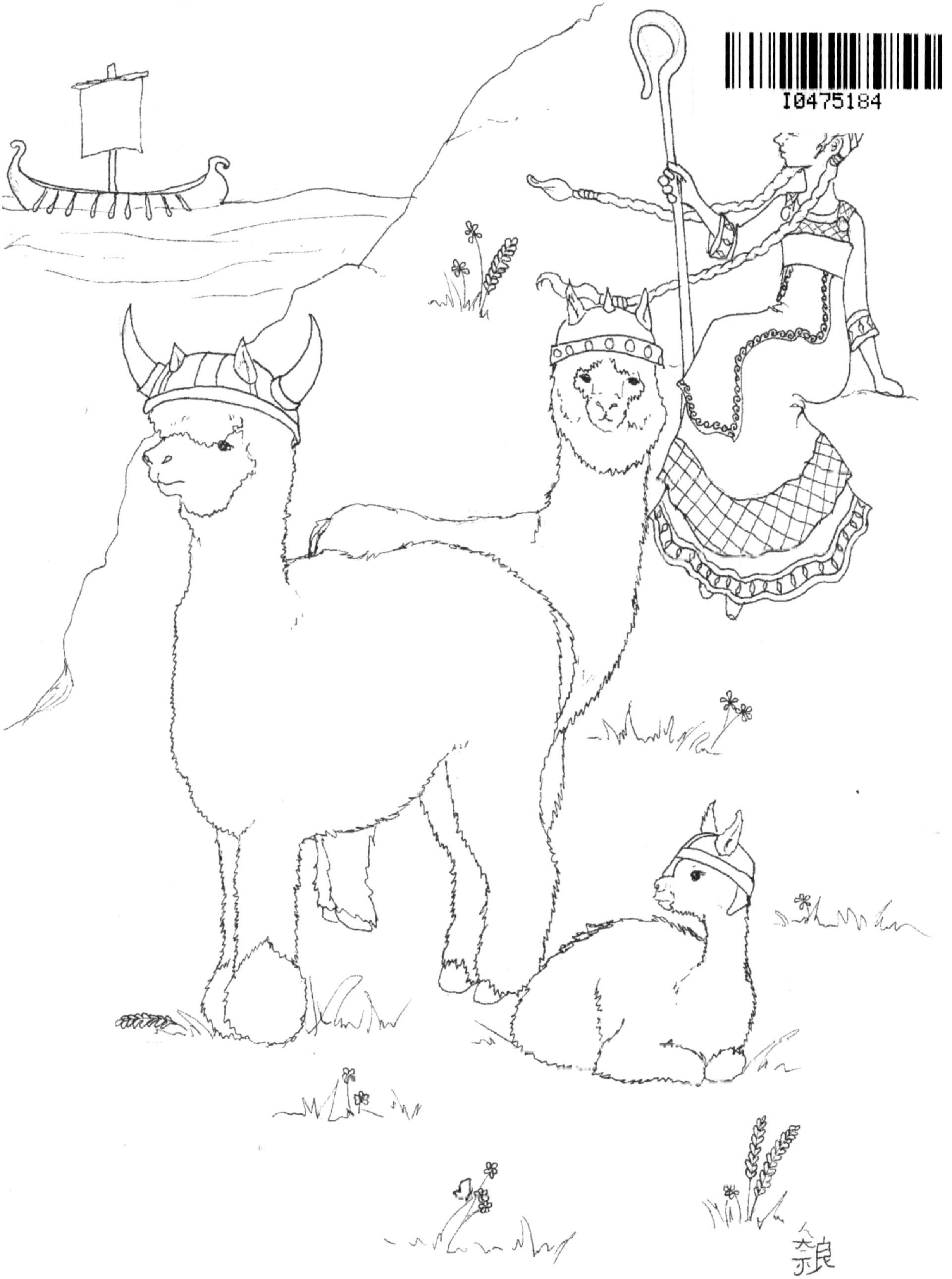
奈良

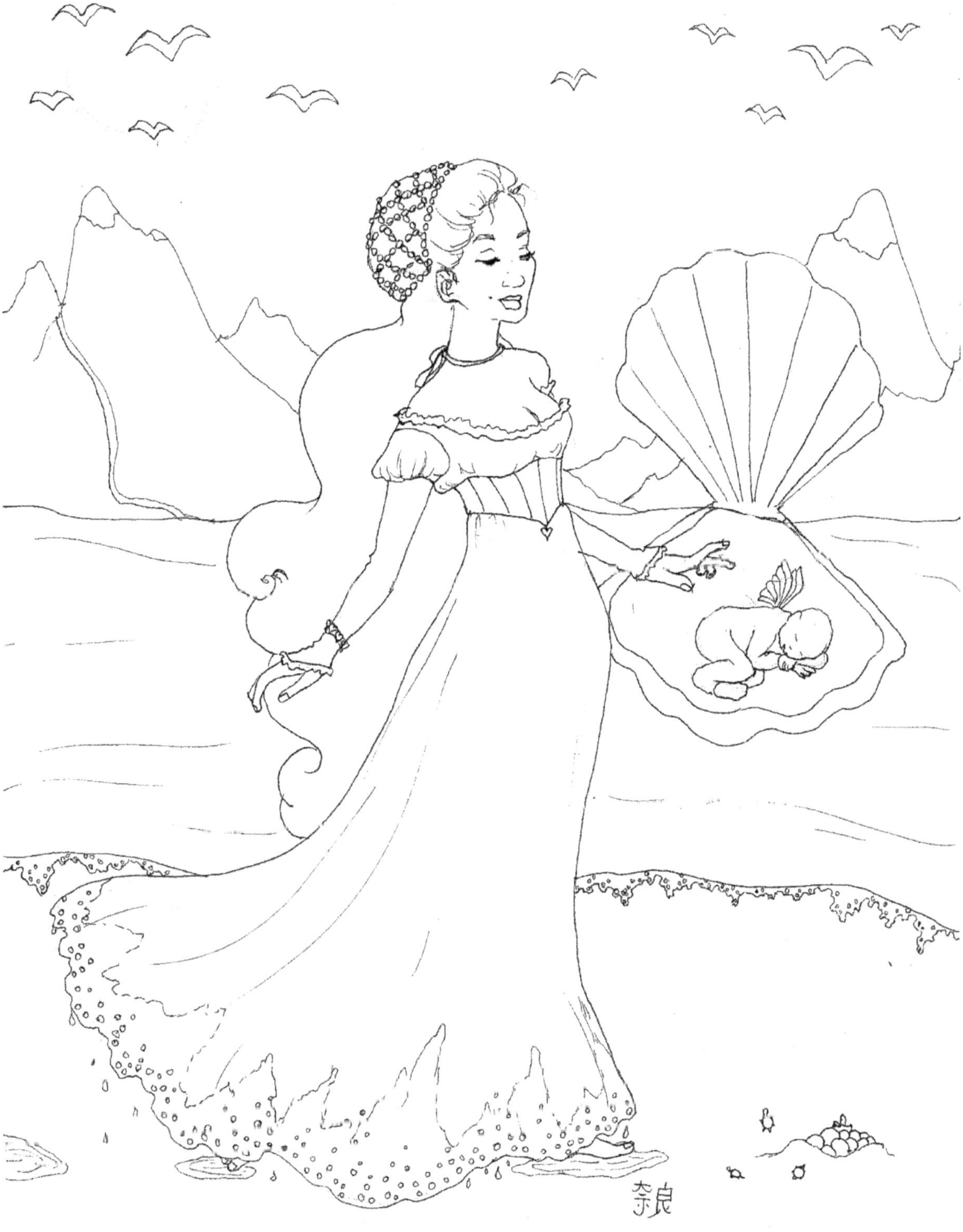
奈良

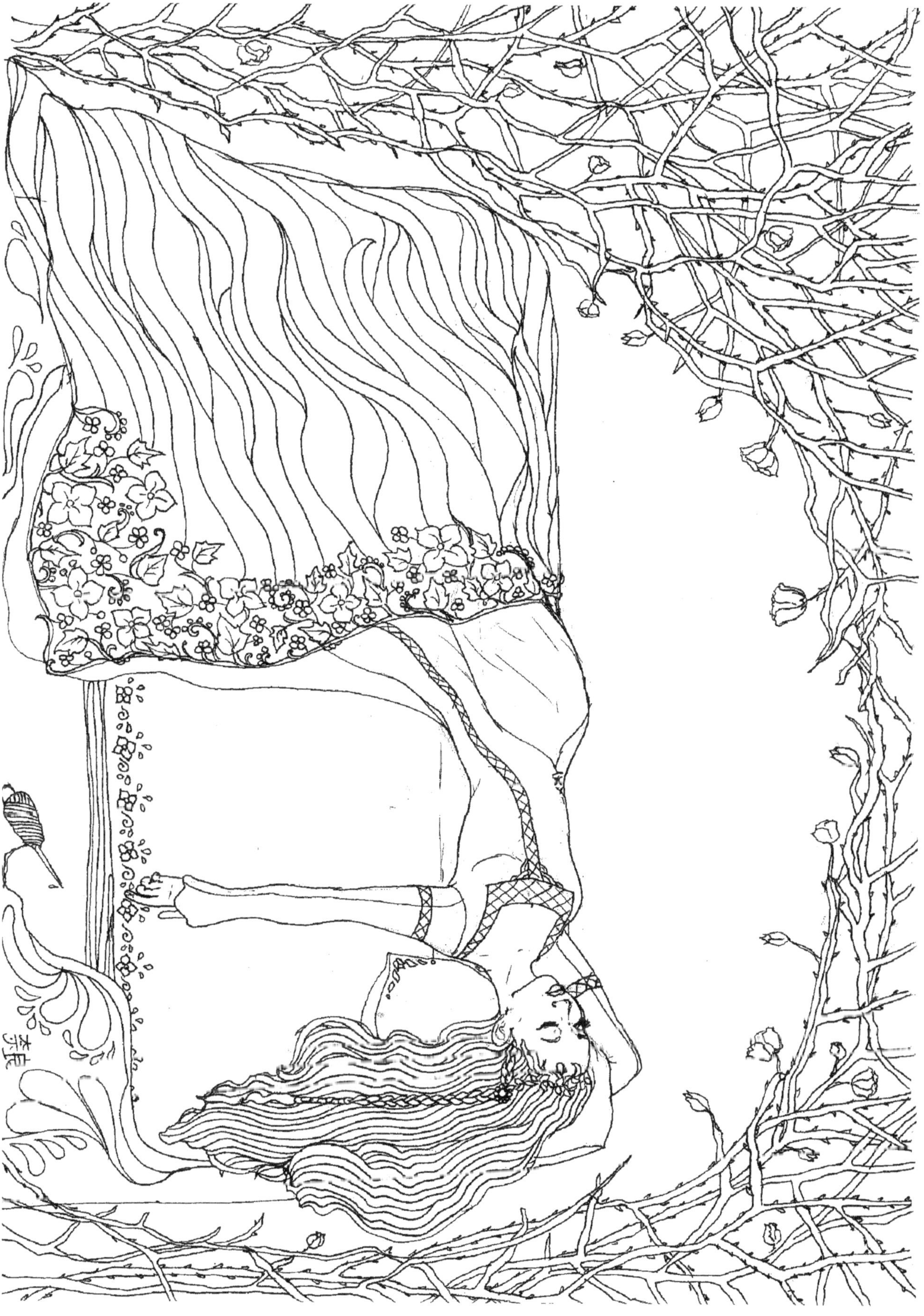

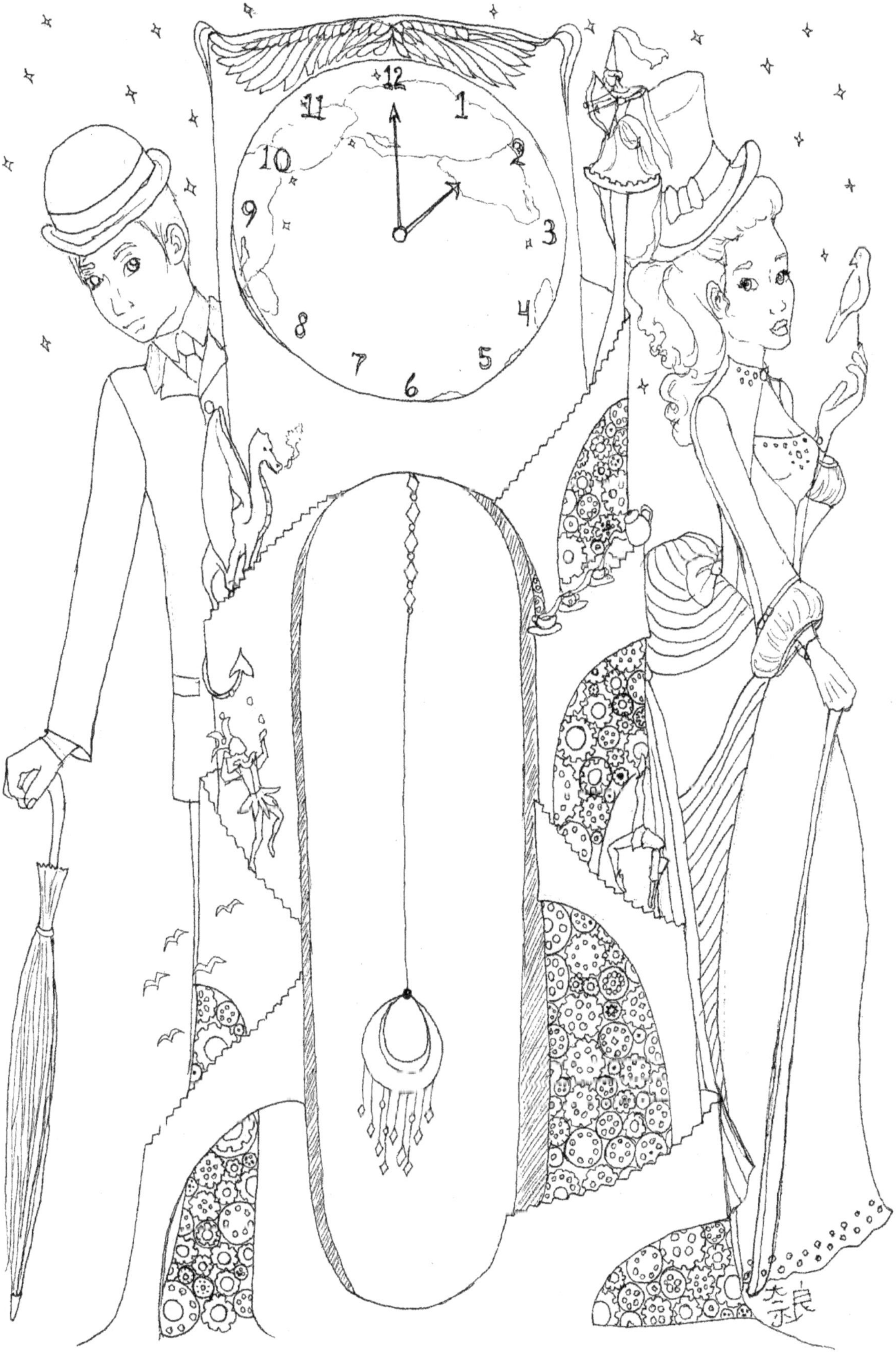

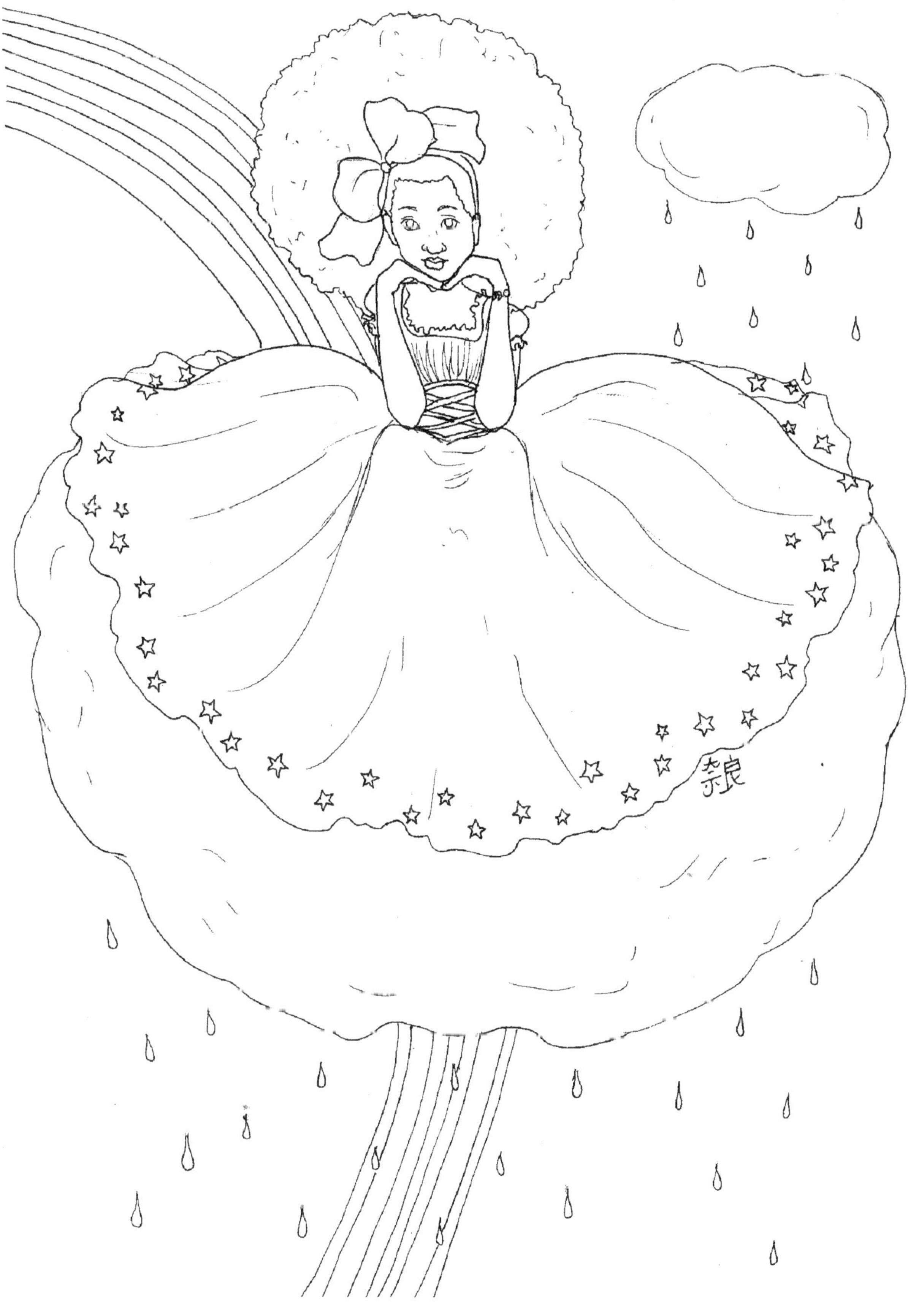

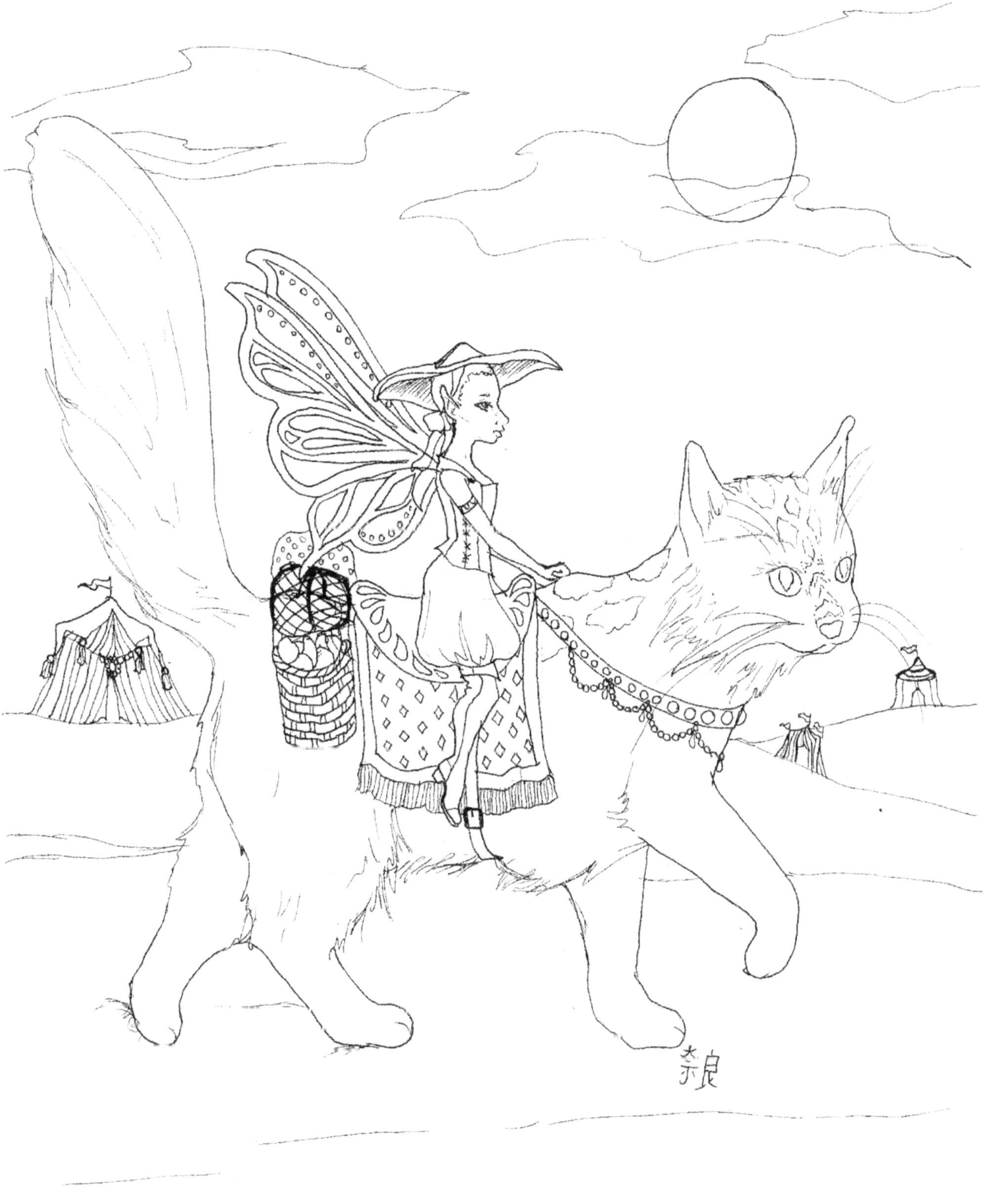
奈良

HAVE YOU CONSIDERED

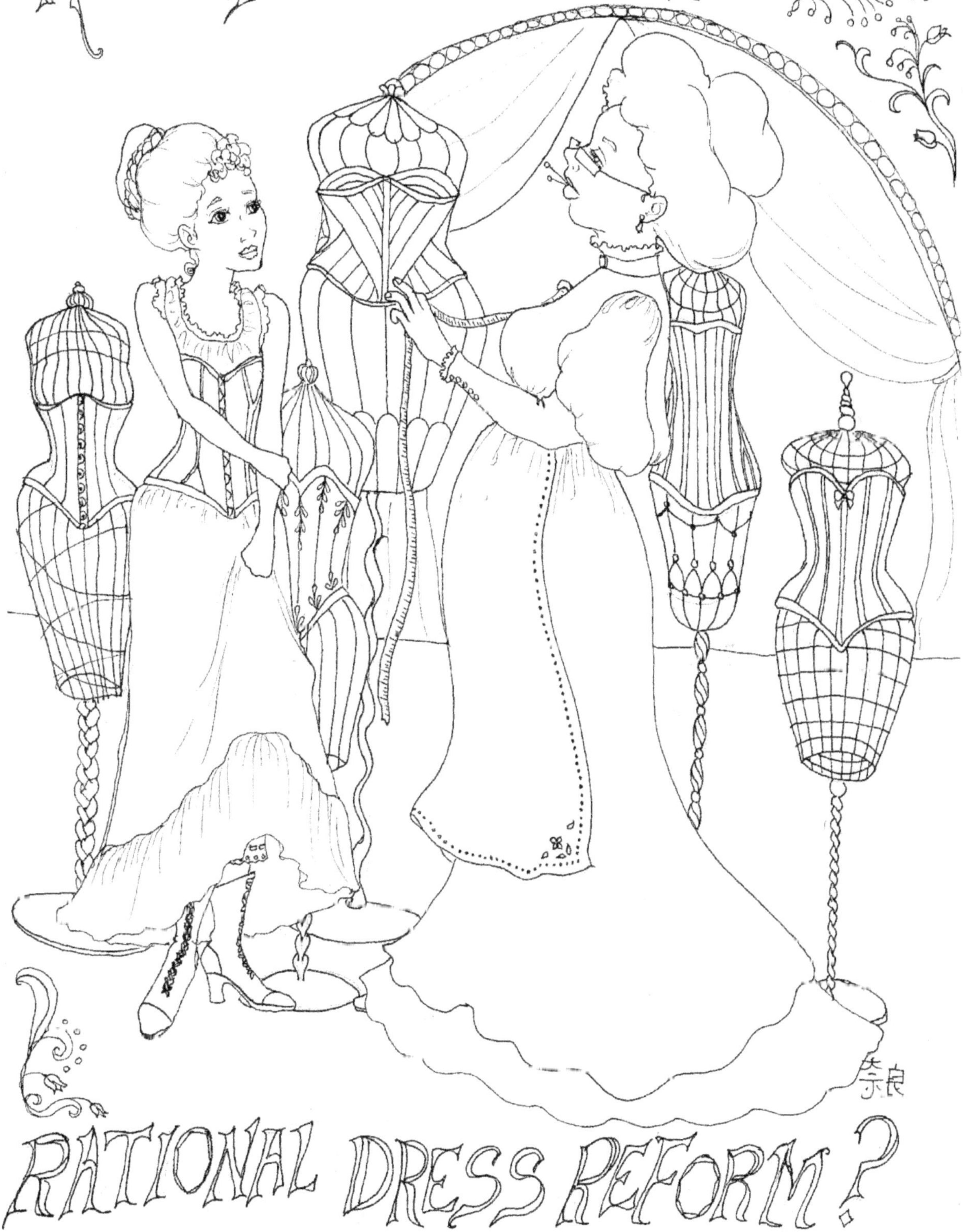

RATIONAL DRESS REFORM?

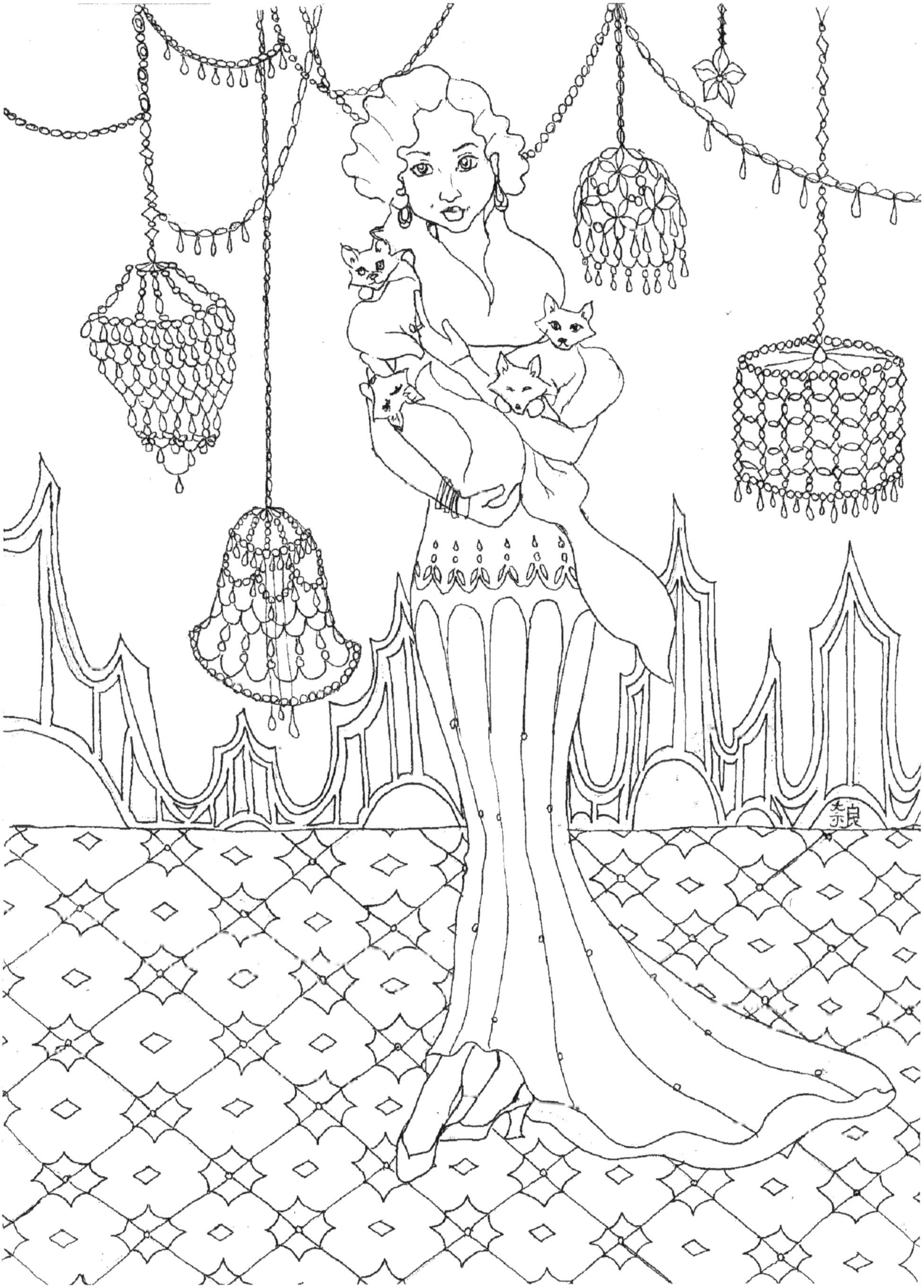

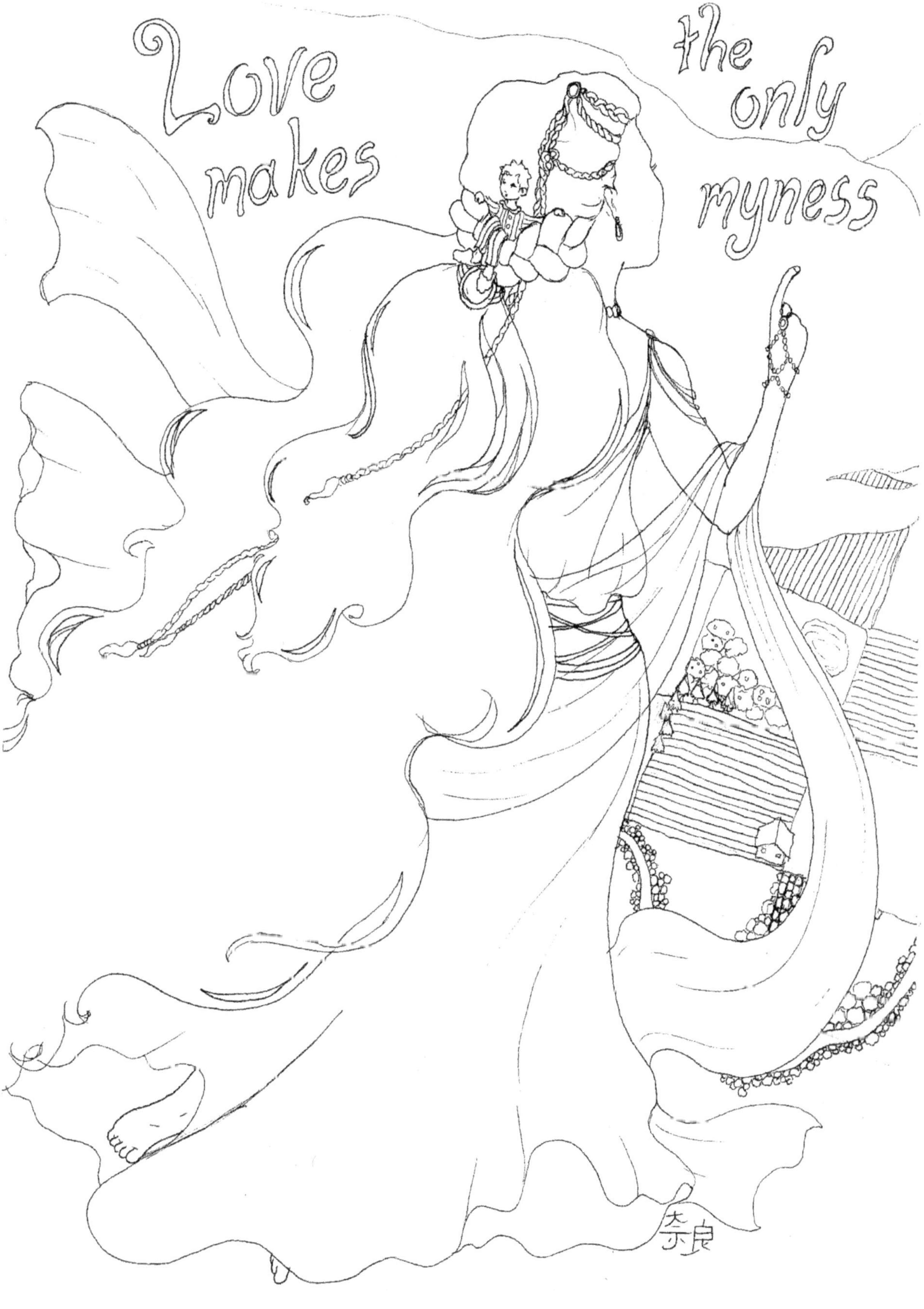
Love makes
the only myness
奈良

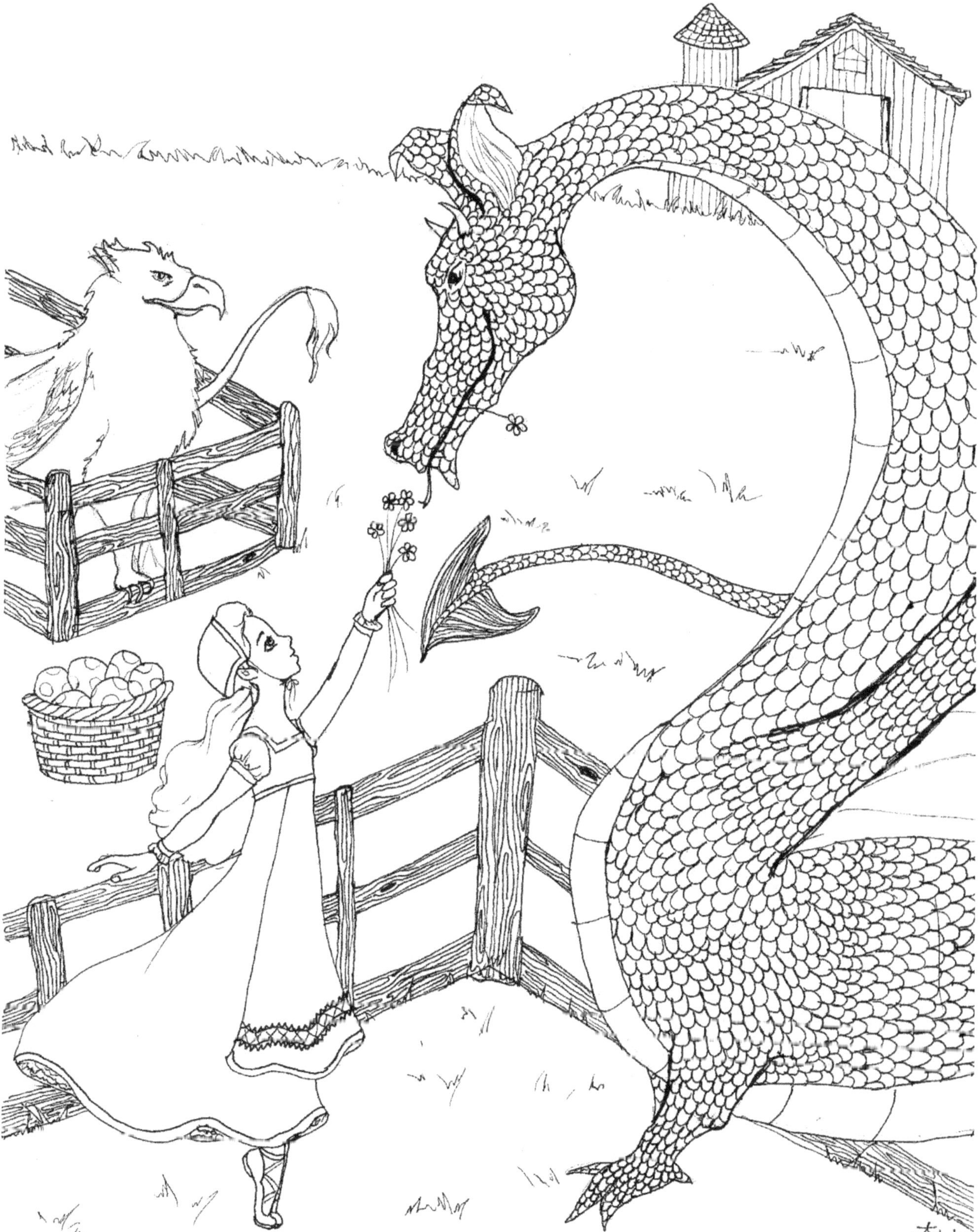

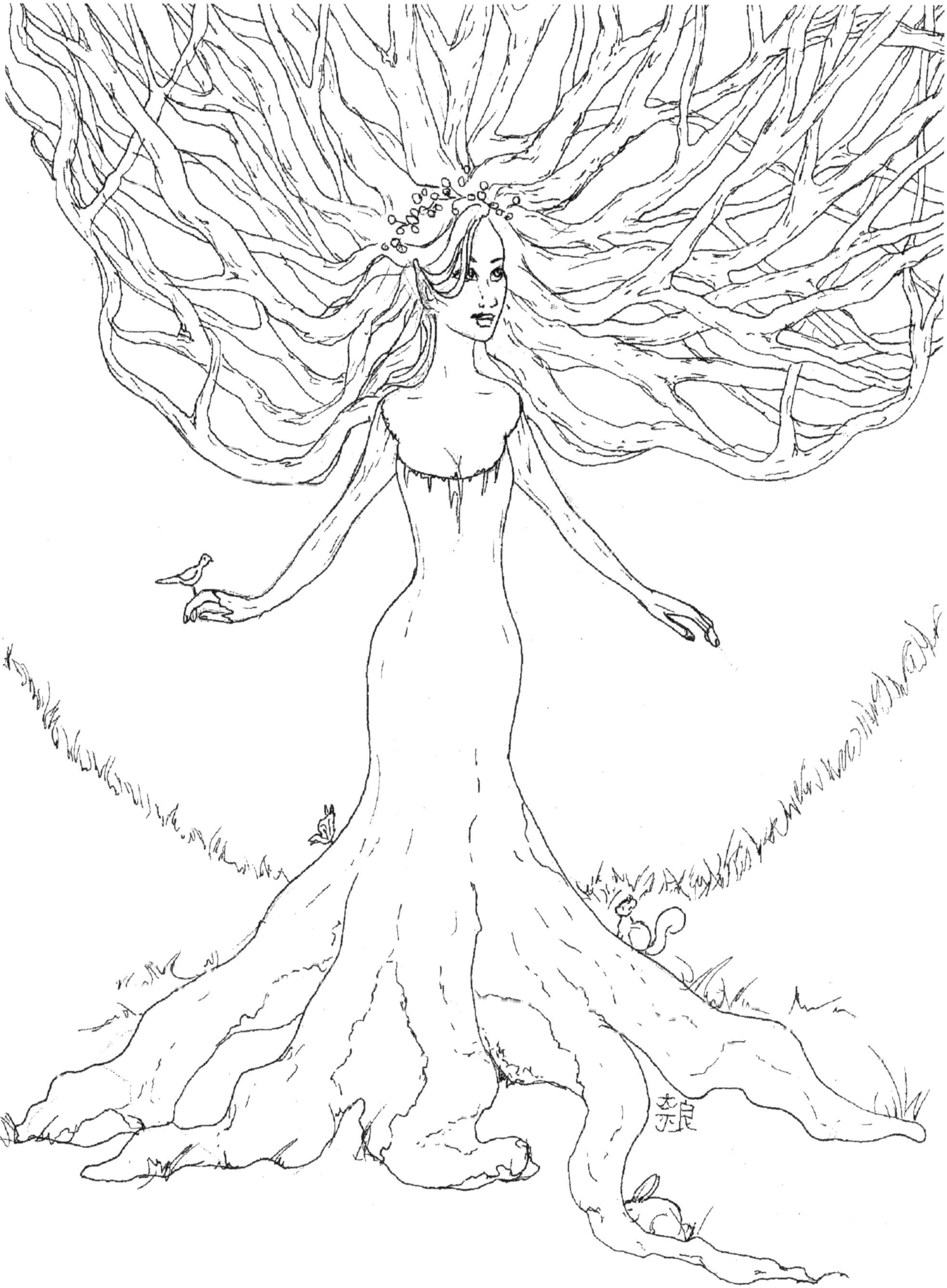

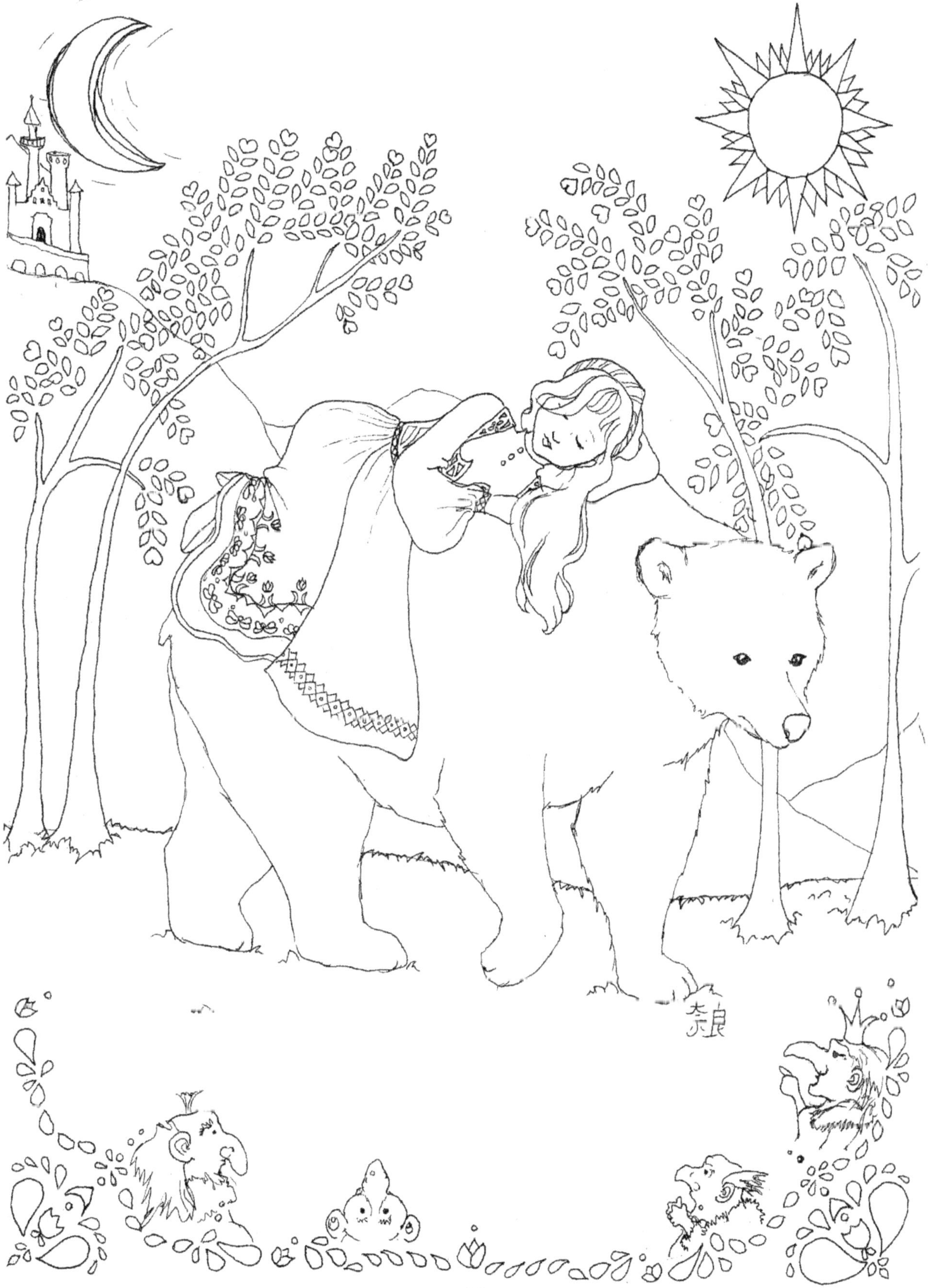

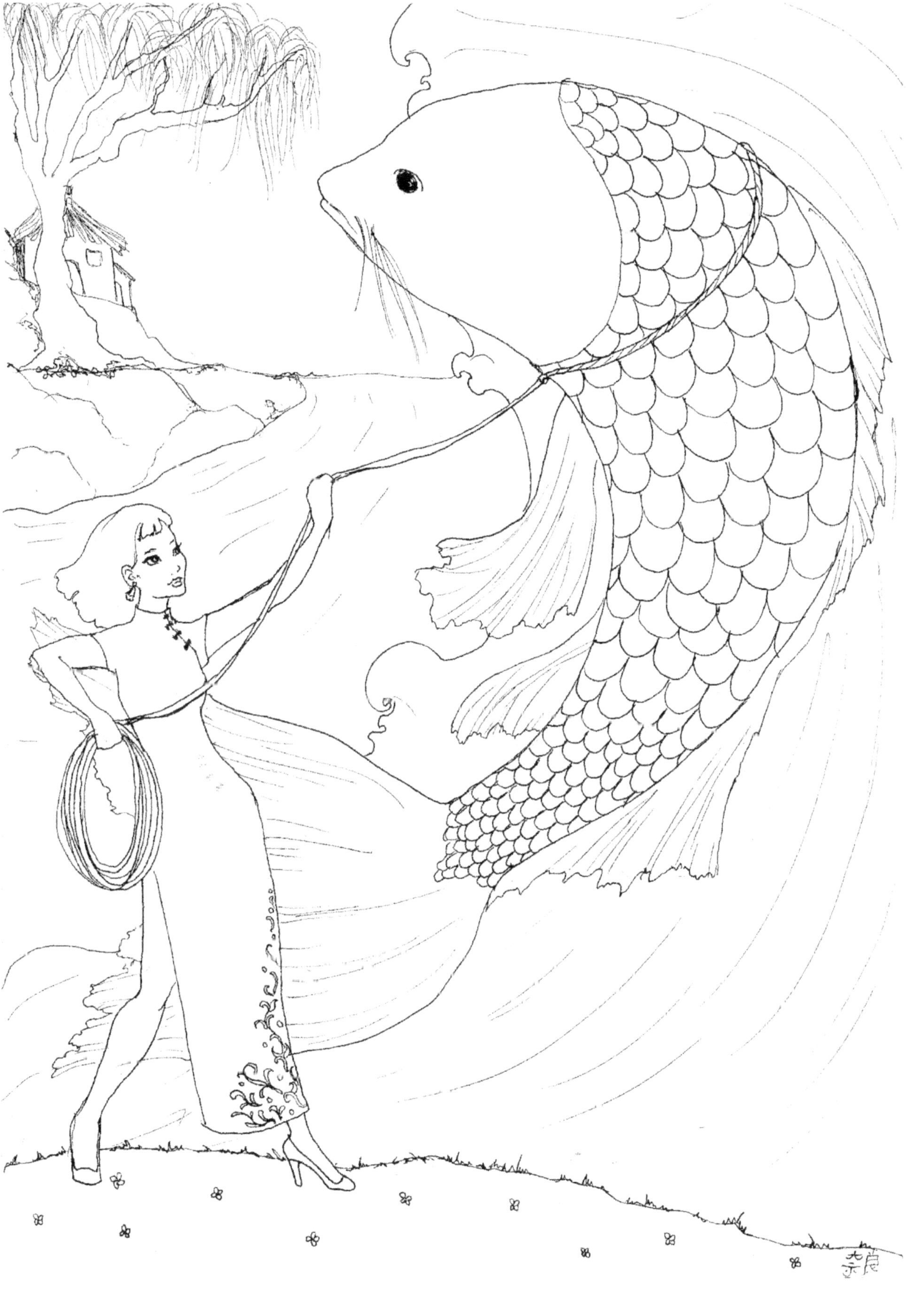

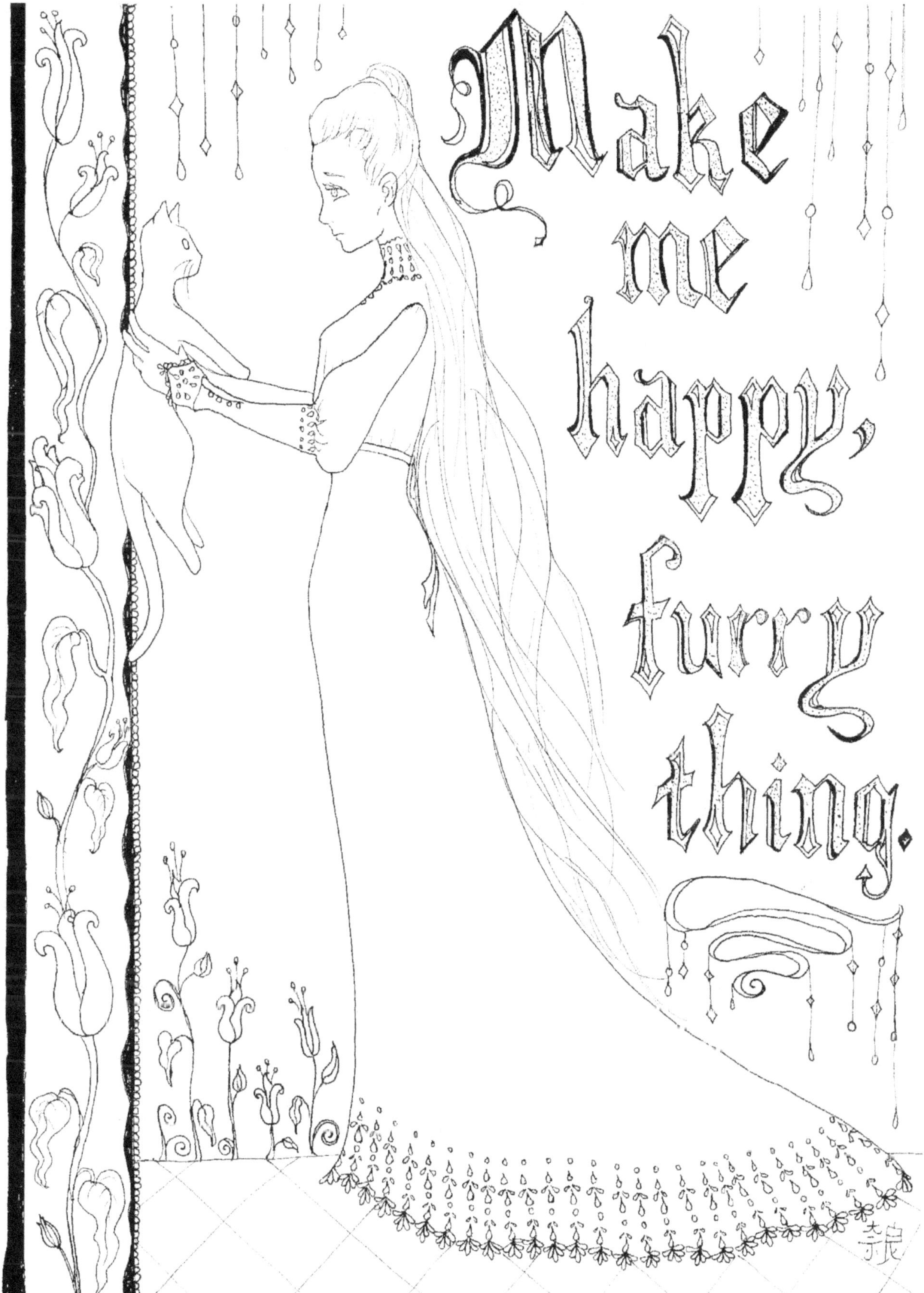
Make me happy, furry thing.

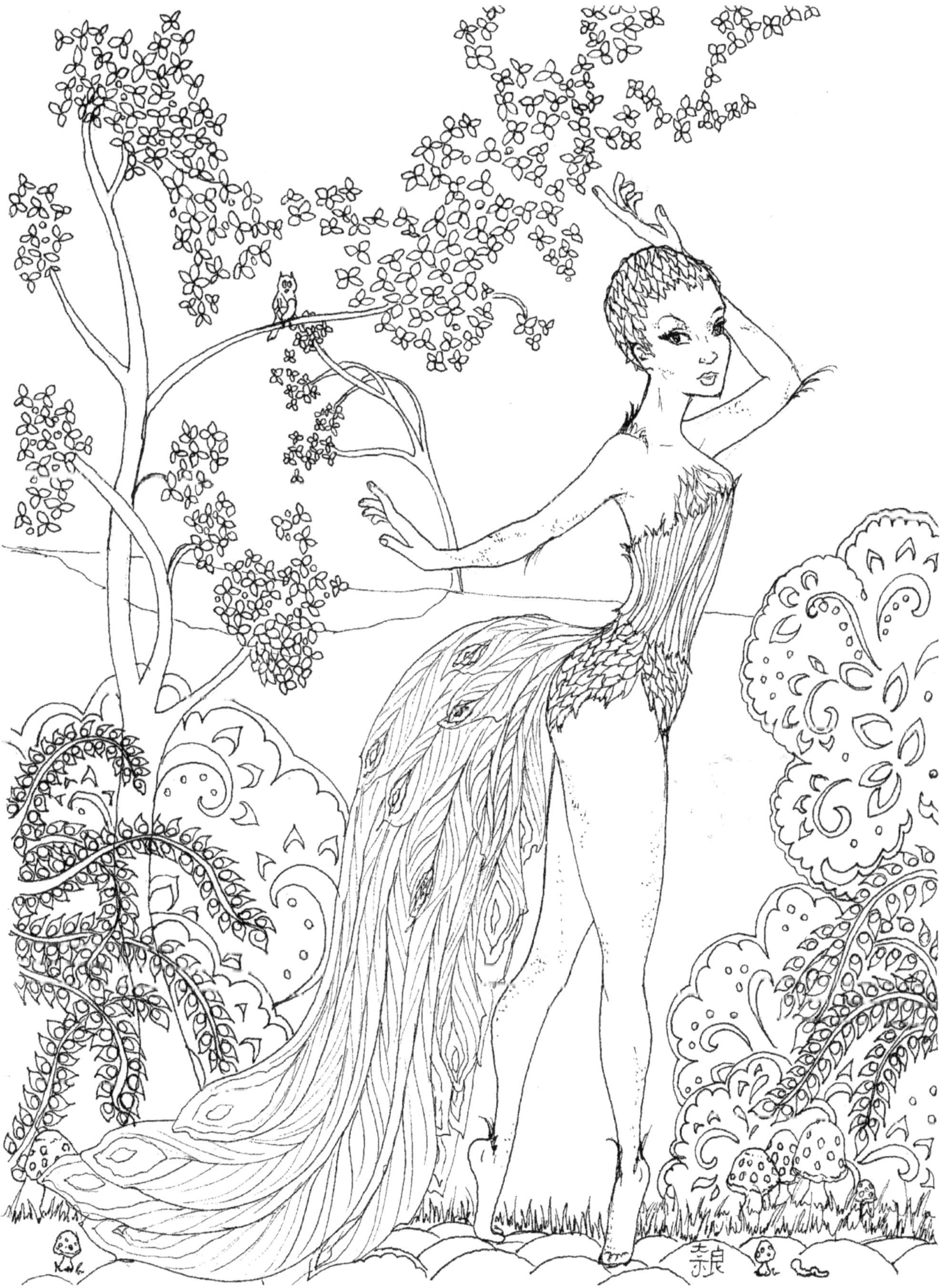

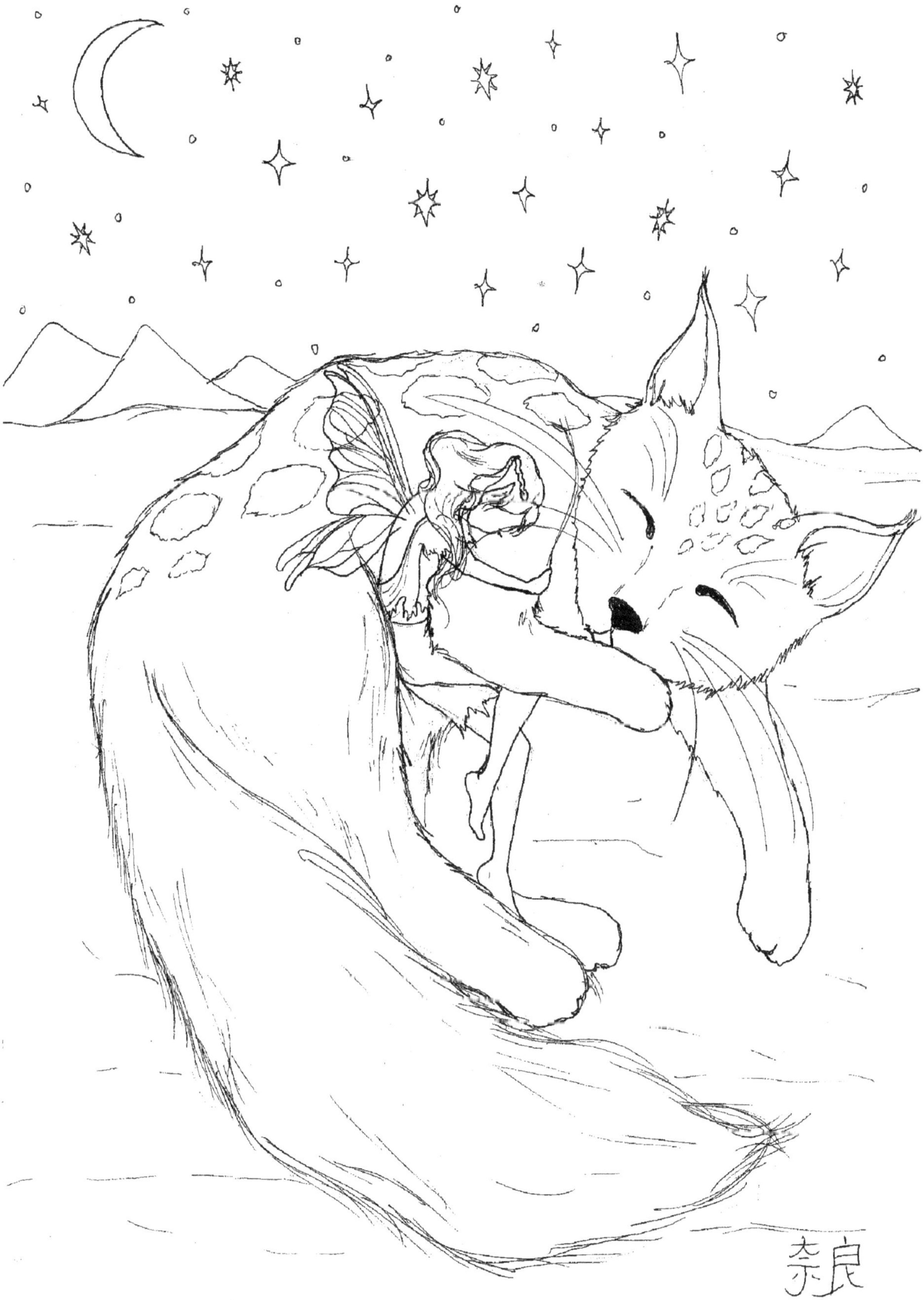
奈良

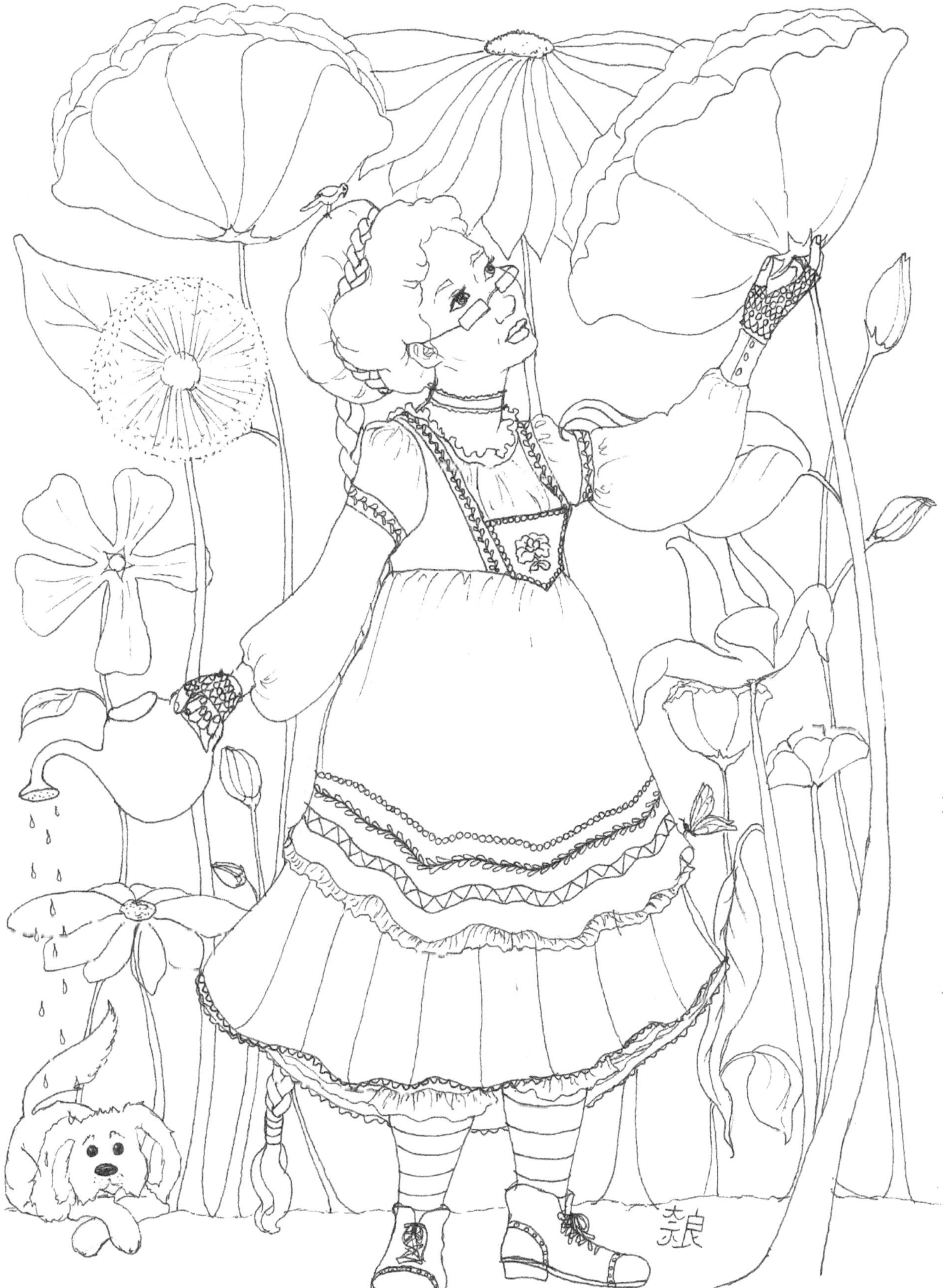

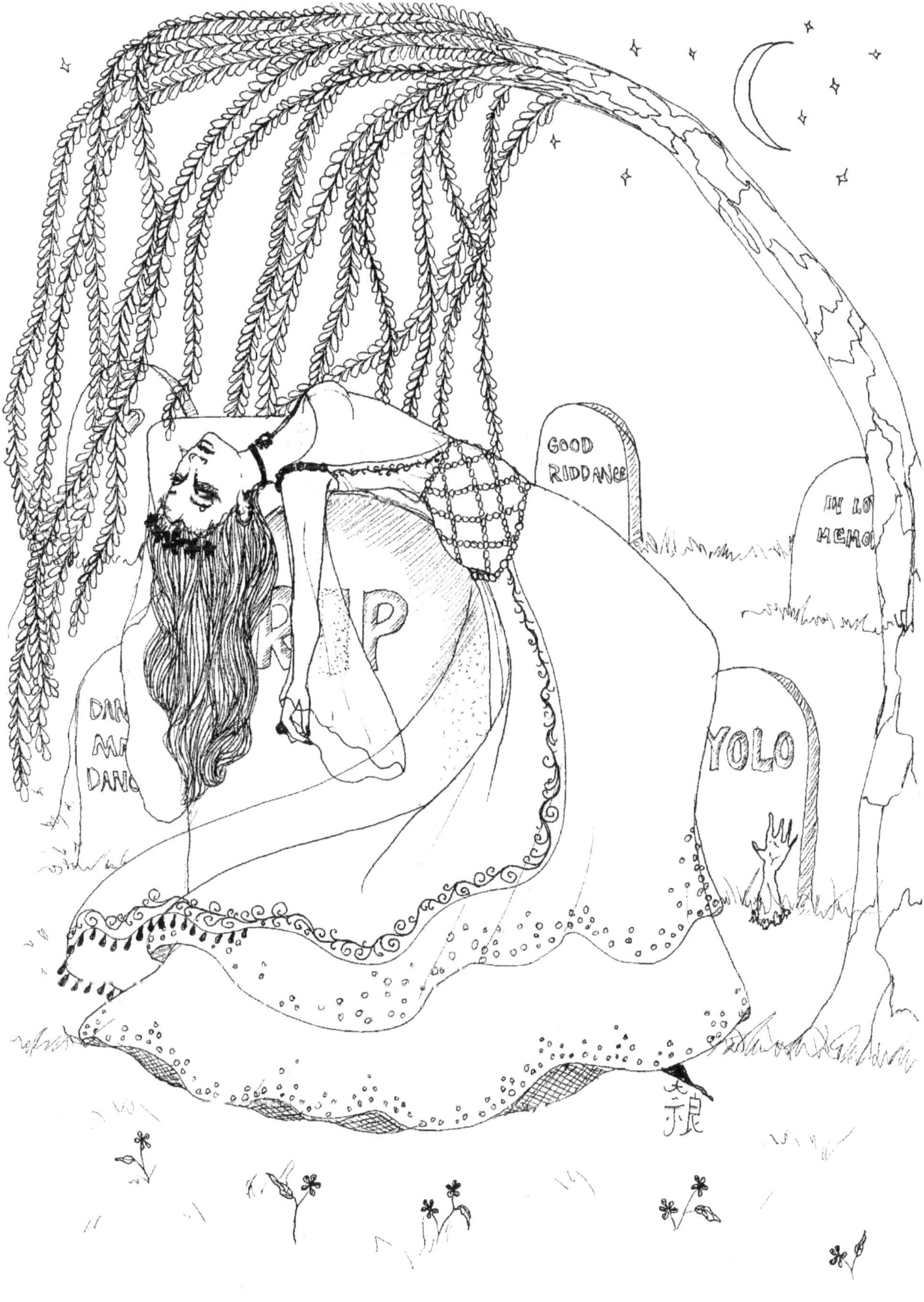
GOOD
RIDDANCE
RIP
YOLO

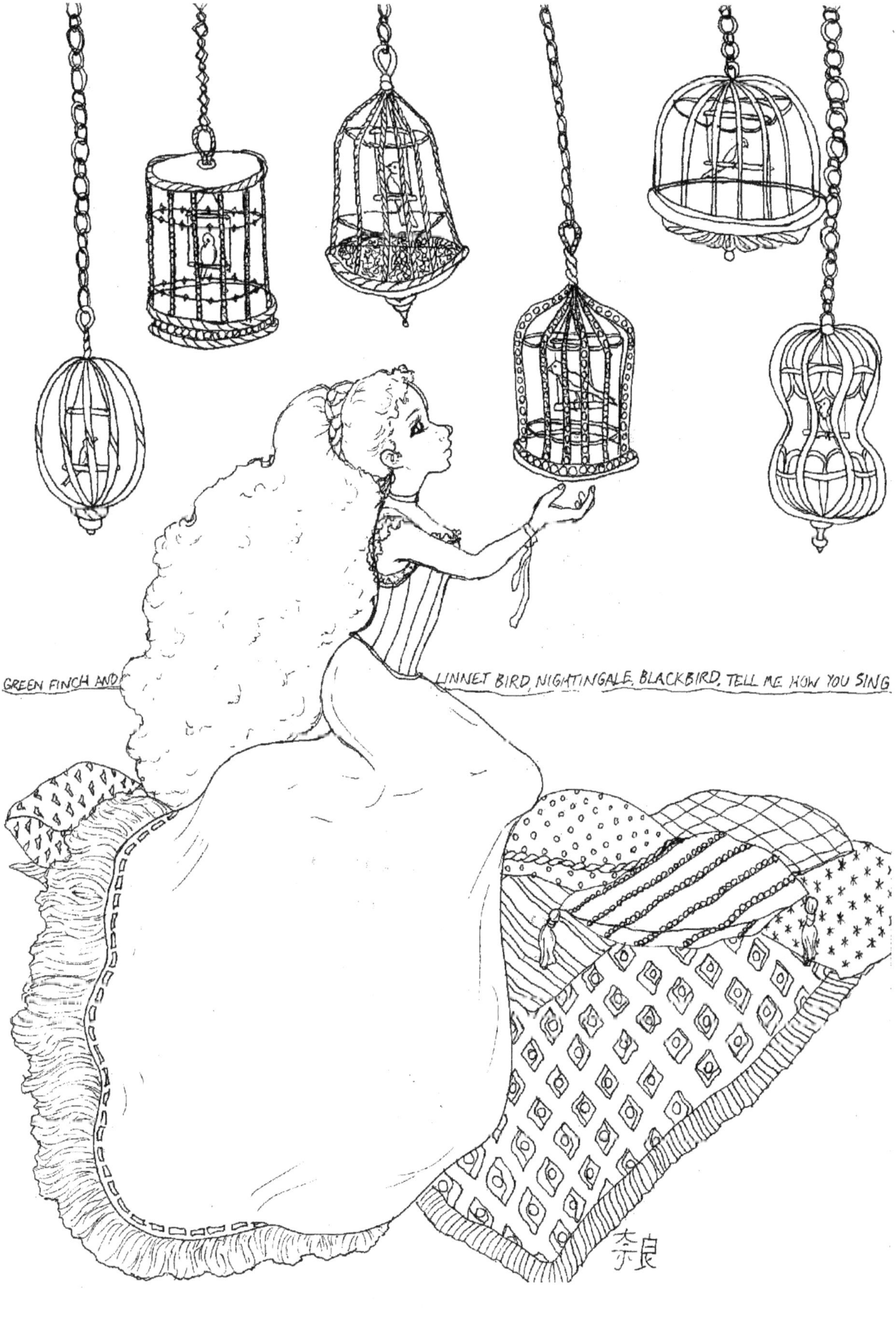
GREEN FINCH AND LINNET BIRD, NIGHTINGALE, BLACKBIRD, TELL ME HOW YOU SING

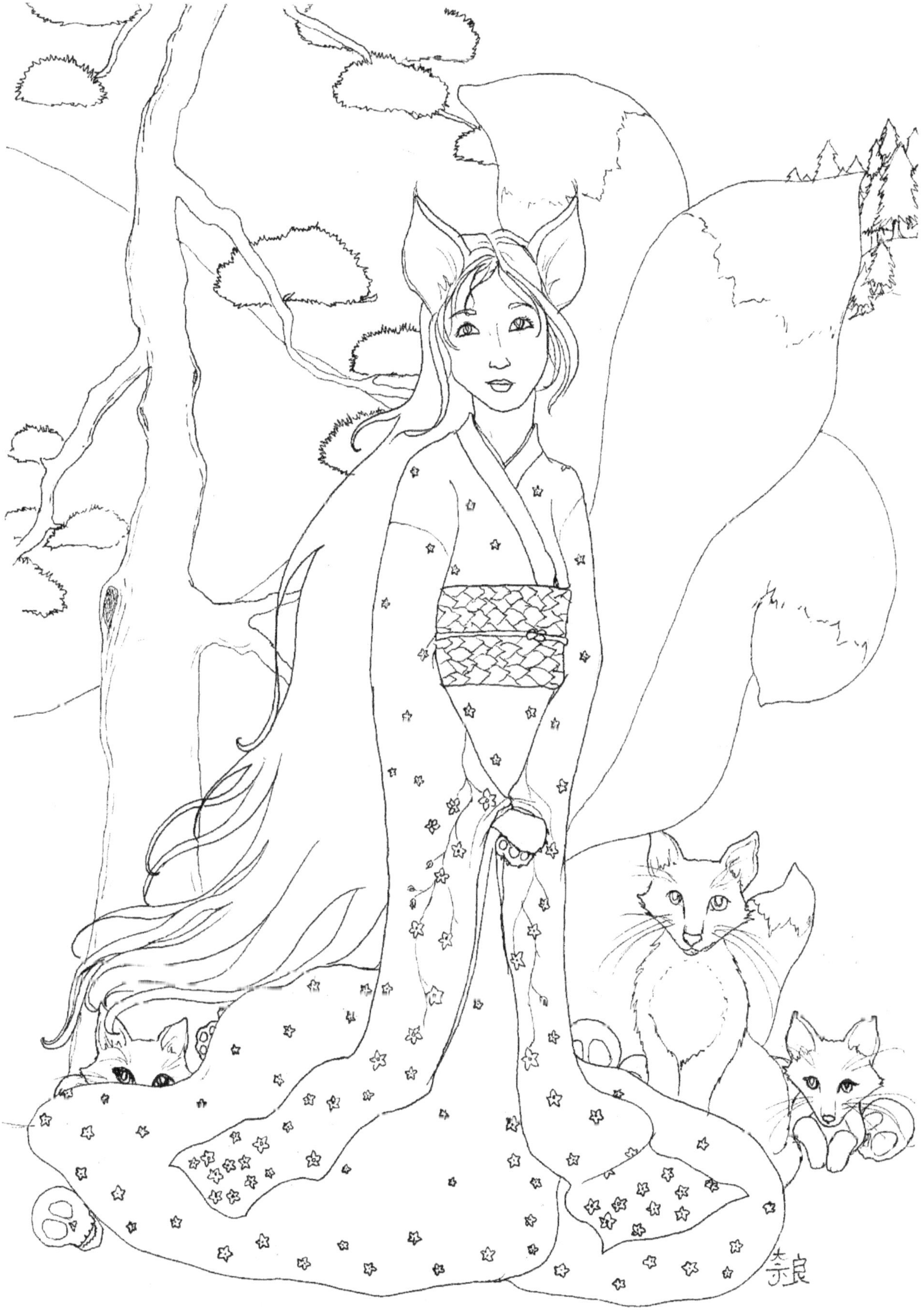
奈良

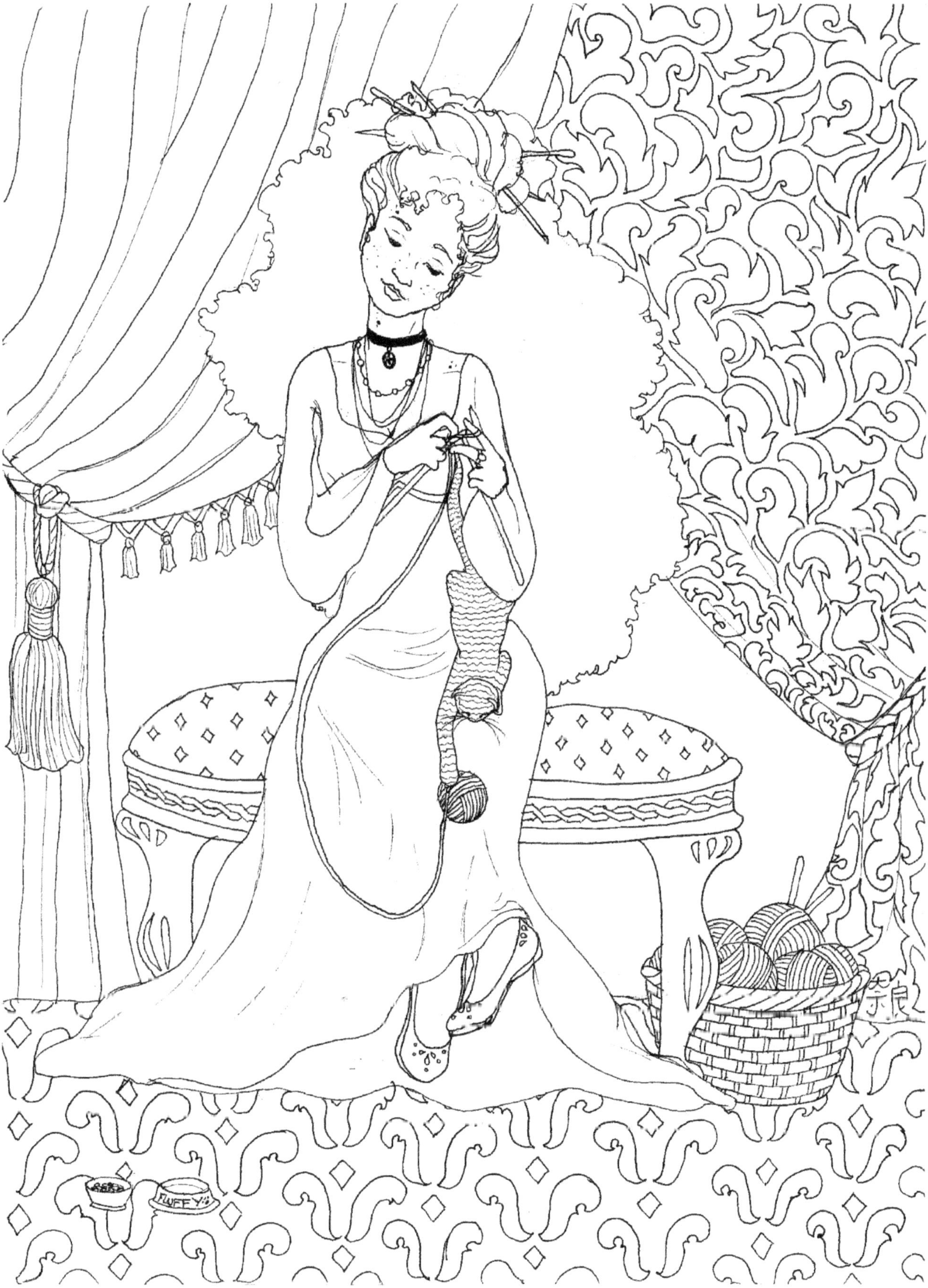
FLUFFY

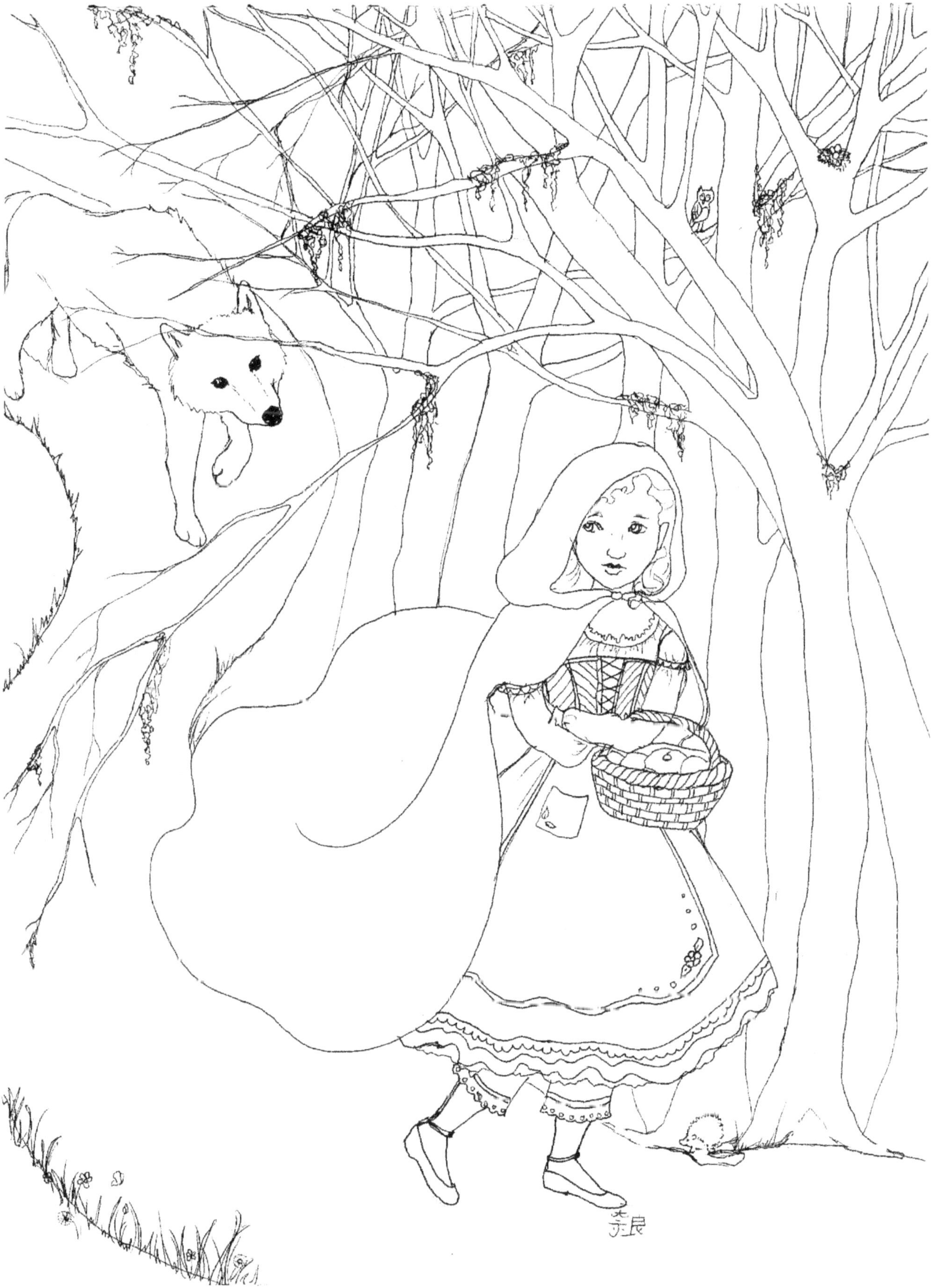

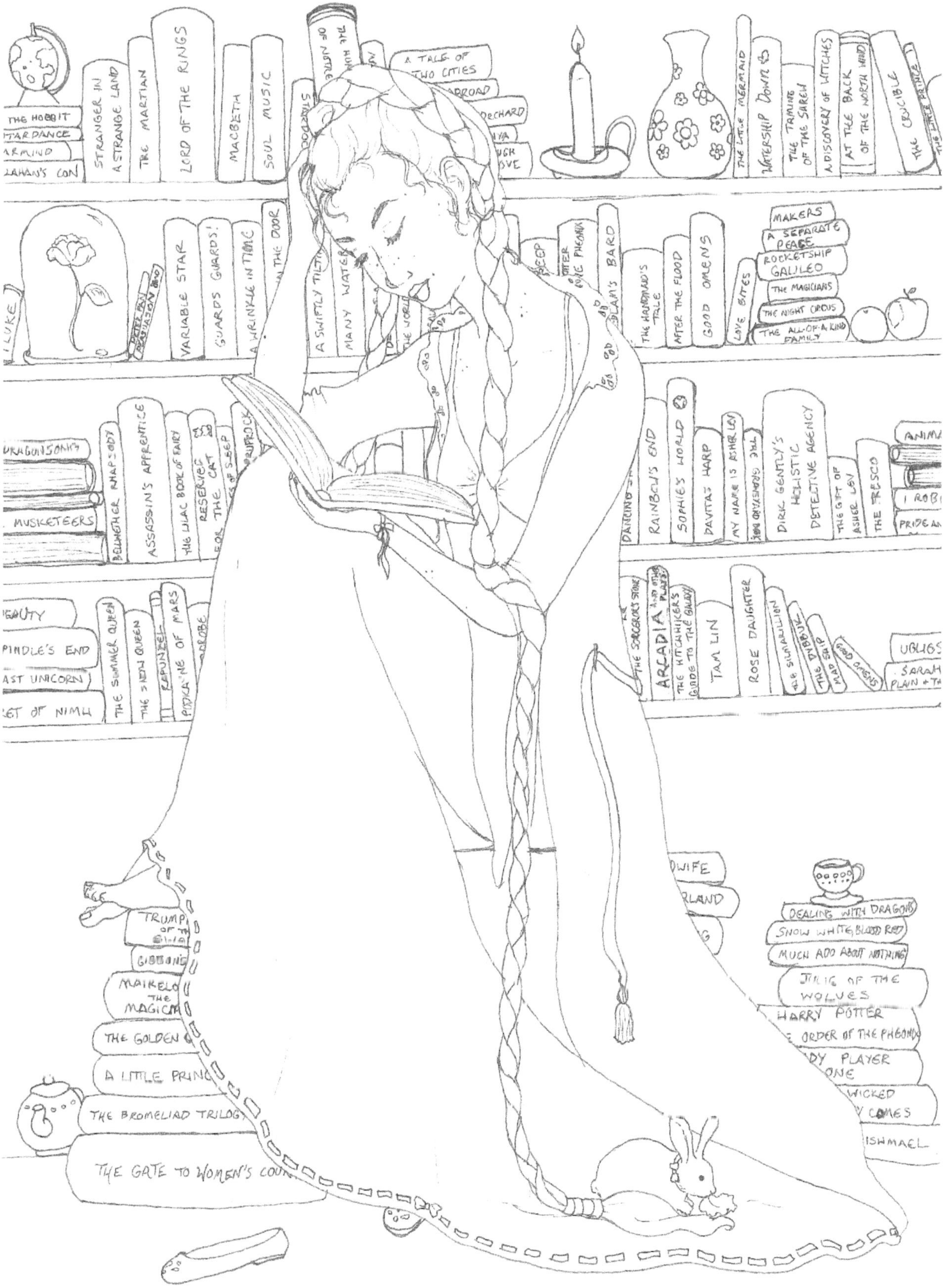
THE HOBBIT
STAR DANCE
STRANGER IN A STRANGE LAND
THE MARTIAN
LORD OF THE RINGS
MACBETH
SOUL MUSIC
A TALE OF TWO CITIES
THE LITTLE MERMAID
WATERSHIP DOWN
THE TAMING OF THE SHREW
A DISCOVERY OF WITCHES
AT THE BACK OF THE NORTH WIND
THE CRUCIBLE
THE LITTLE PRINCE
VARIABLE STAR
GUARDS GUARDS!
A WRINKLE IN TIME
A SWIFTLY TILTING
MANY WATERS
THE HANDMAID'S TALE
AFTER THE FLOOD
GOOD OMENS
LOVE BITES
MAKERS
A SEPARATE PEACE
ROCKETSHIP GALILEO
THE MAGICIANS
THE NIGHT CIRCUS
THE ALL-OF-A-KIND FAMILY
DRAGONSONG
MUSKETEERS
BELLWETHER RHAPSODY
ASSASSIN'S APPRENTICE
THE LILAC BOOK OF FAIRY
RESERVED FOR THE CAT
RAINBOW'S END
SOPHIE'S WORLD
DAVITA'S HARP
MY NAME IS ASHER LEV
DIRK GENTLY'S HOLISTIC DETECTIVE AGENCY
THE GIFT OF ASHER LEV
THE FRESCO
I ROBOT
PRIDE AN
BEAUTY
SPINDLE'S END
LAST UNICORN
SECRET OF NIMH
THE SUMMER QUEEN
THE SNOW QUEEN
RAPUNZEL
PRINCESS OF MARS
ARCADIA
THE HITCHHIKER'S GUIDE TO THE GALAXY
TAM LIN
ROSE DAUGHTER
THE SILMARILLION
THE DYBBUK
MAD SHIP
GOOD OMENS
SARAH PLAIN & TALL
TRUMPET OF THE SWAN
GIBBONS
MAIRELON THE MAGICIAN
THE GOLDEN
A LITTLE PRINCE
THE BROMELIAD TRILOGY
THE GATE TO WOMEN'S COUNTRY
DEALING WITH DRAGONS
SNOW WHITE BLOOD RED
MUCH ADO ABOUT NOTHING
JULIE OF THE WOLVES
HARRY POTTER
ORDER OF THE PHOENIX
READY PLAYER ONE
WICKED
COMES
ISHMAEL

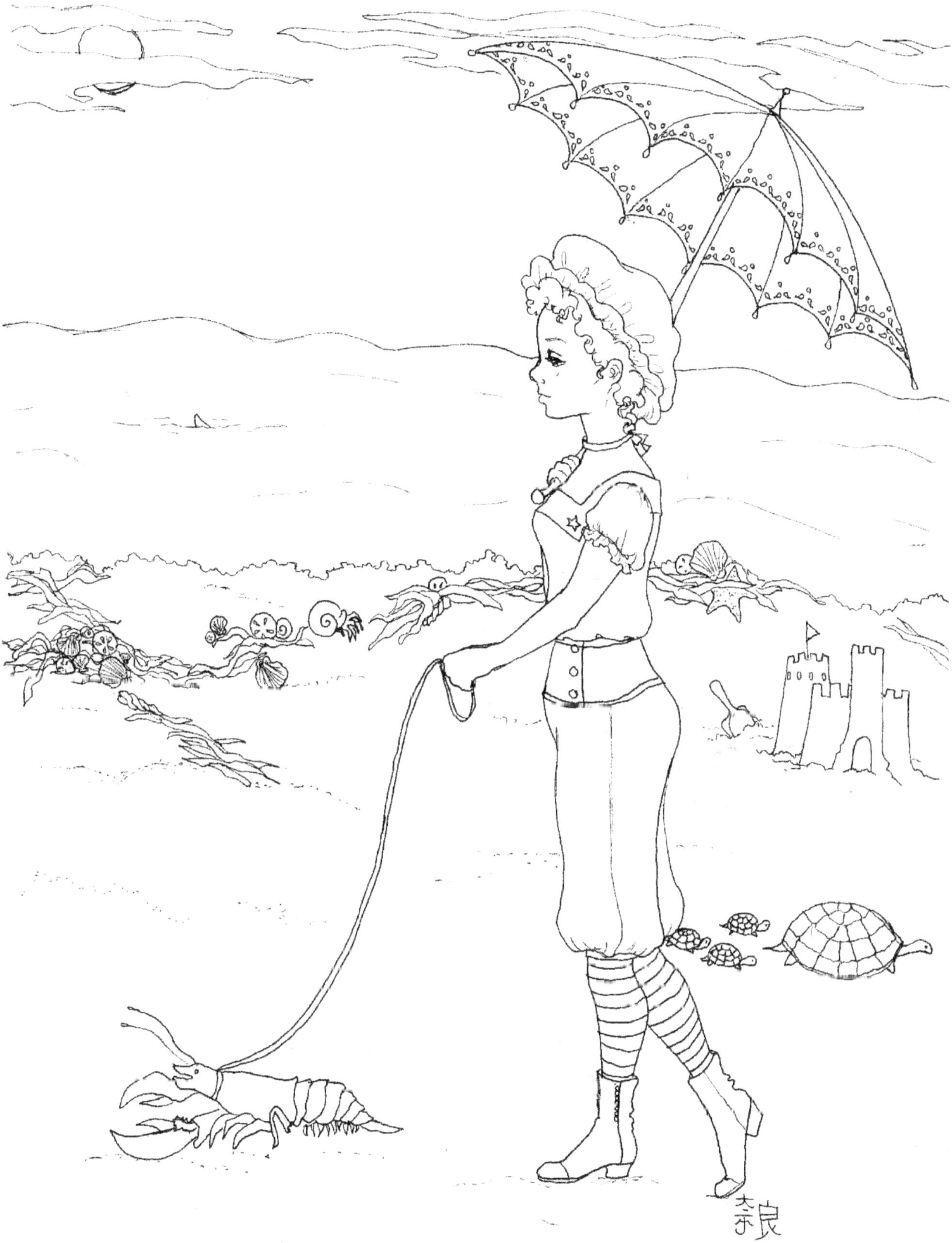
奈良

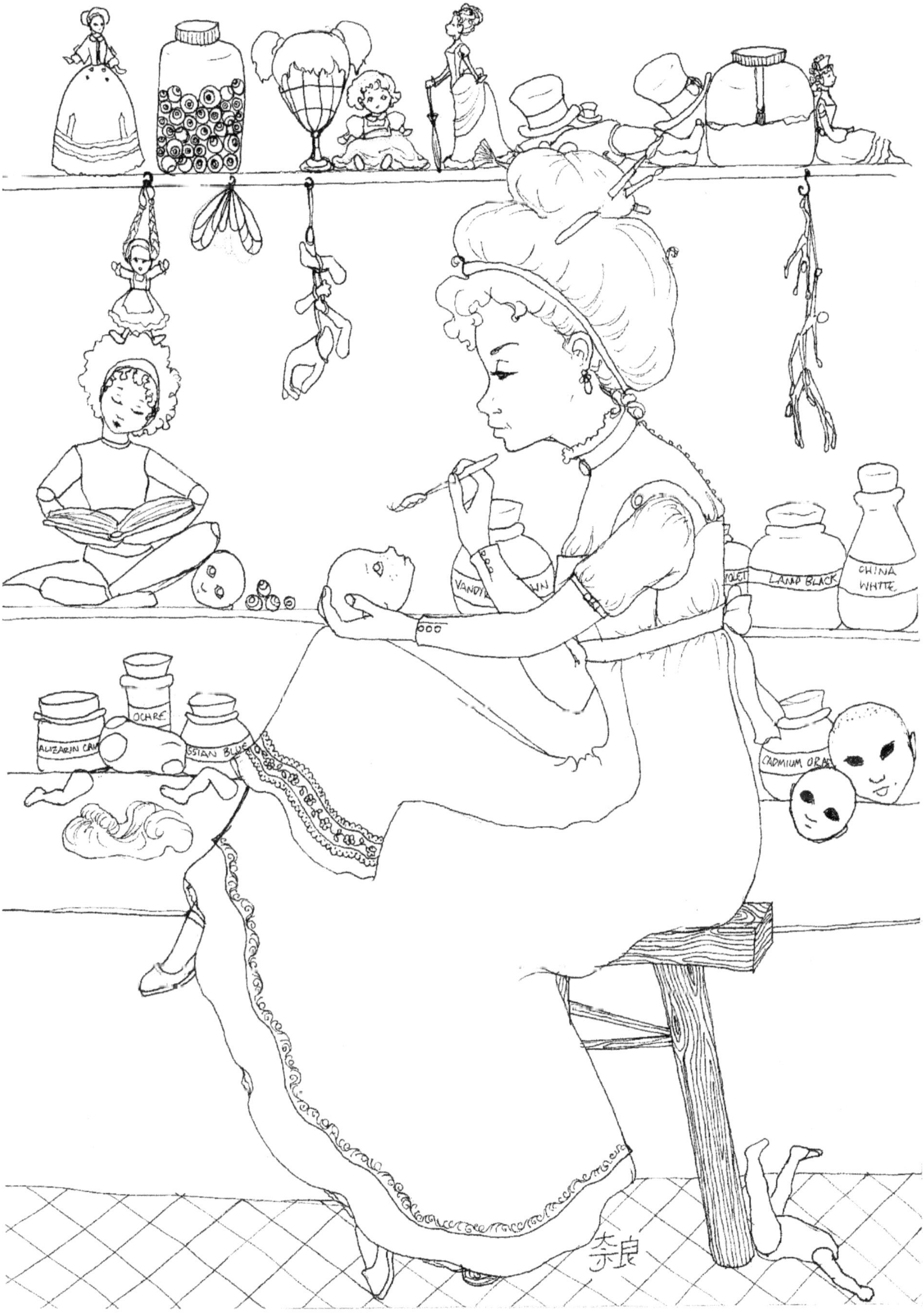
ALIZARIN CRI
OCHRE
SSIAN BLUE
VANDY
WN
IOLET
LAMP BLACK
CHINA WHITE
CADMIUM ORA
奈良

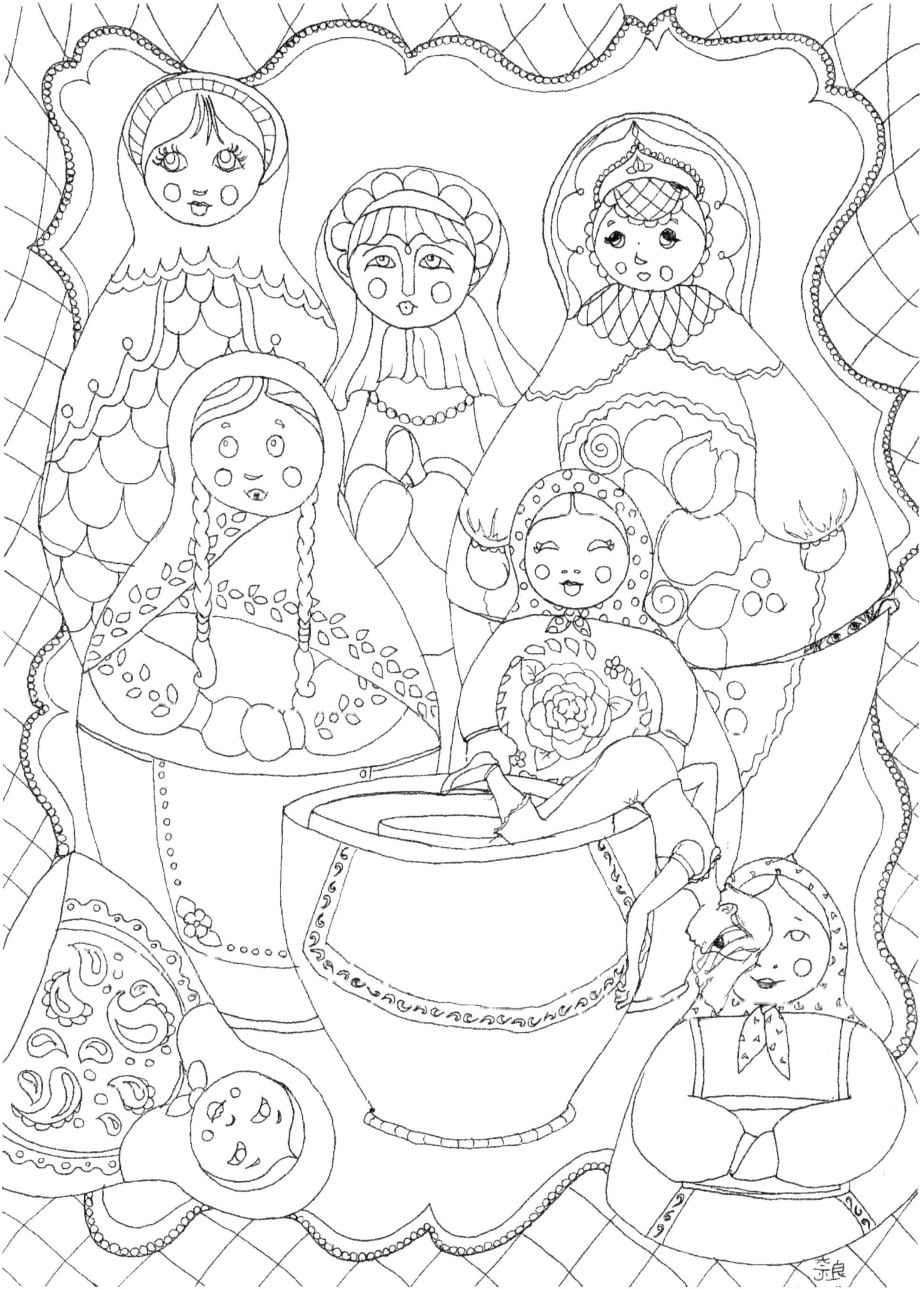

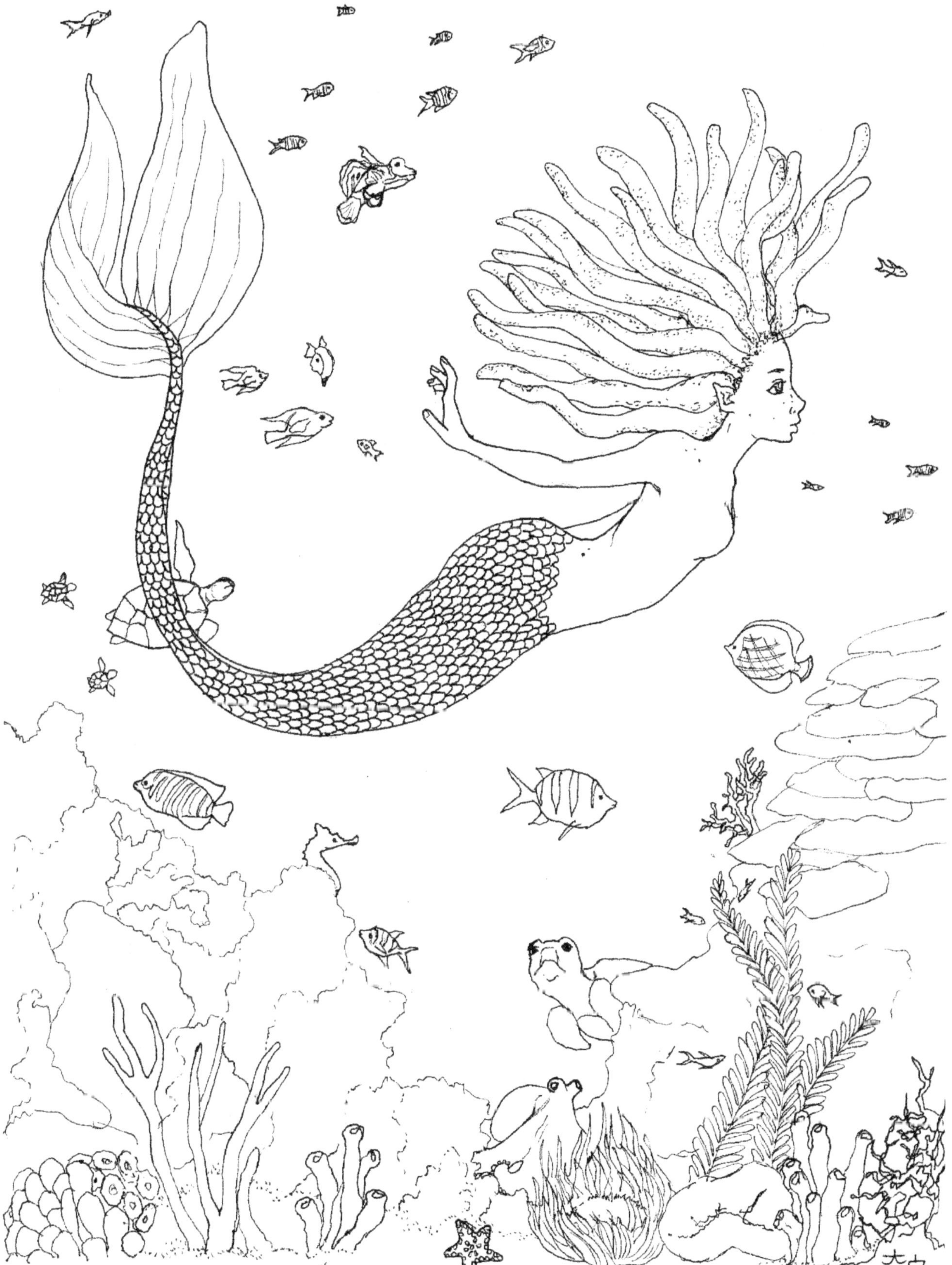

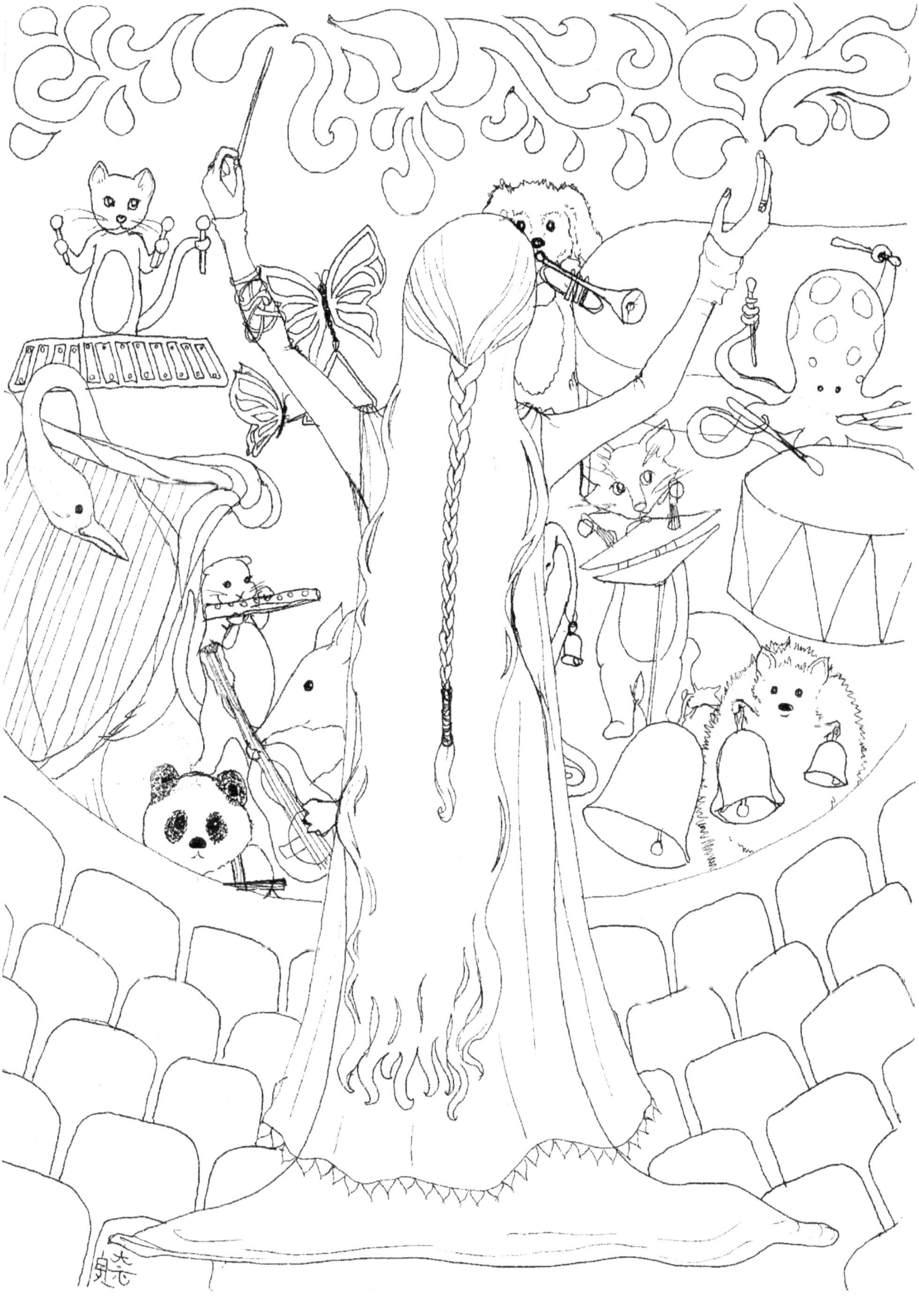

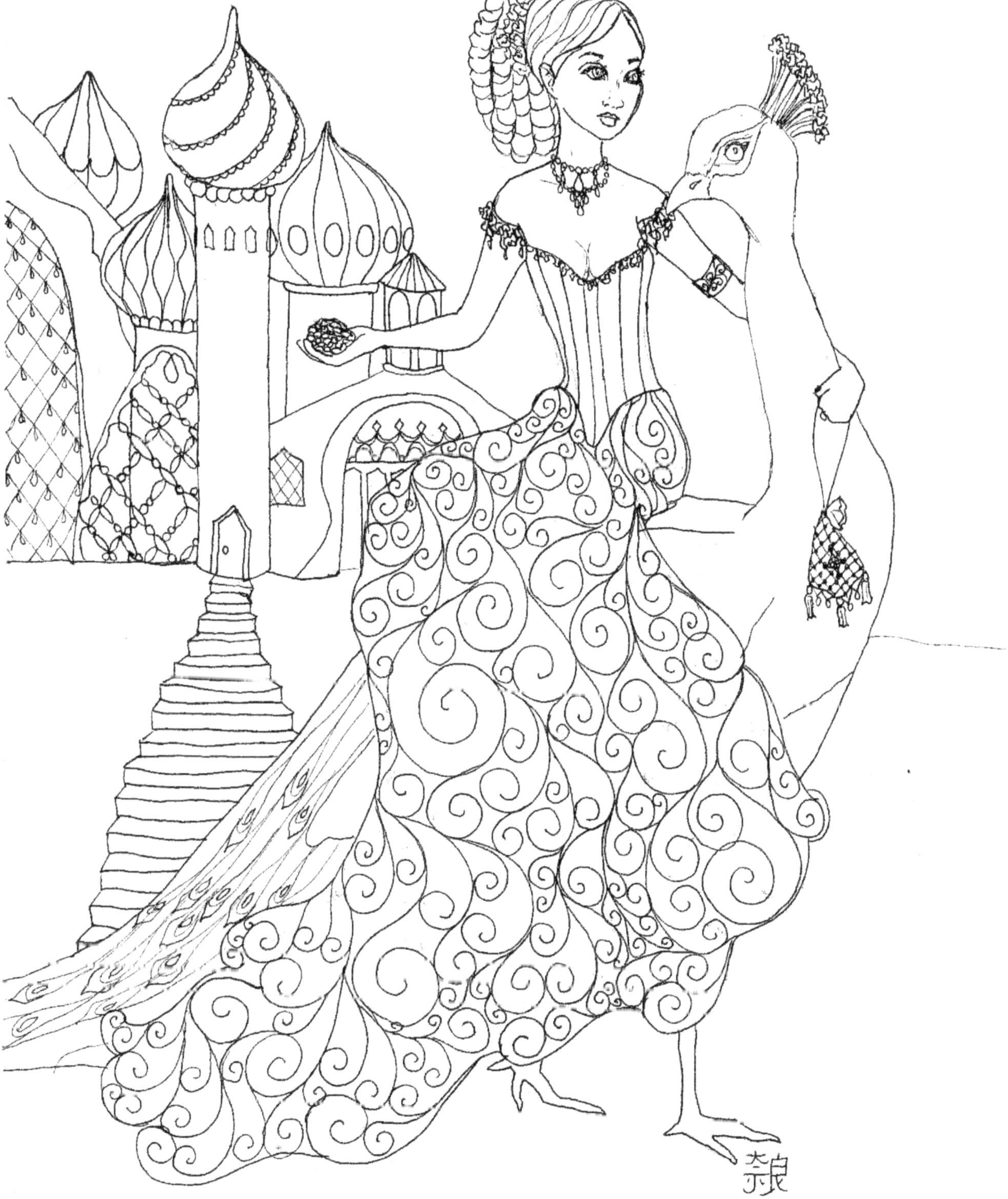

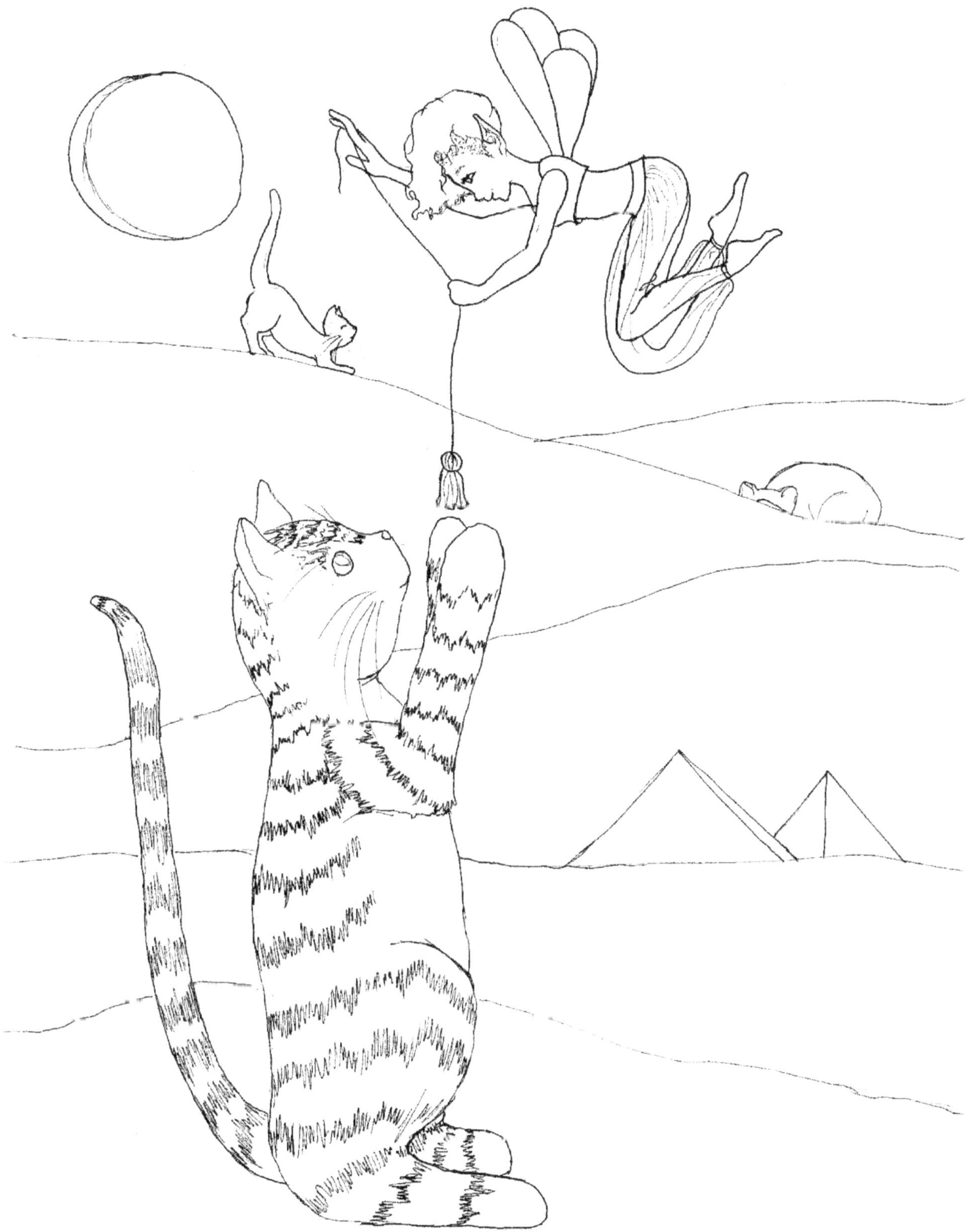

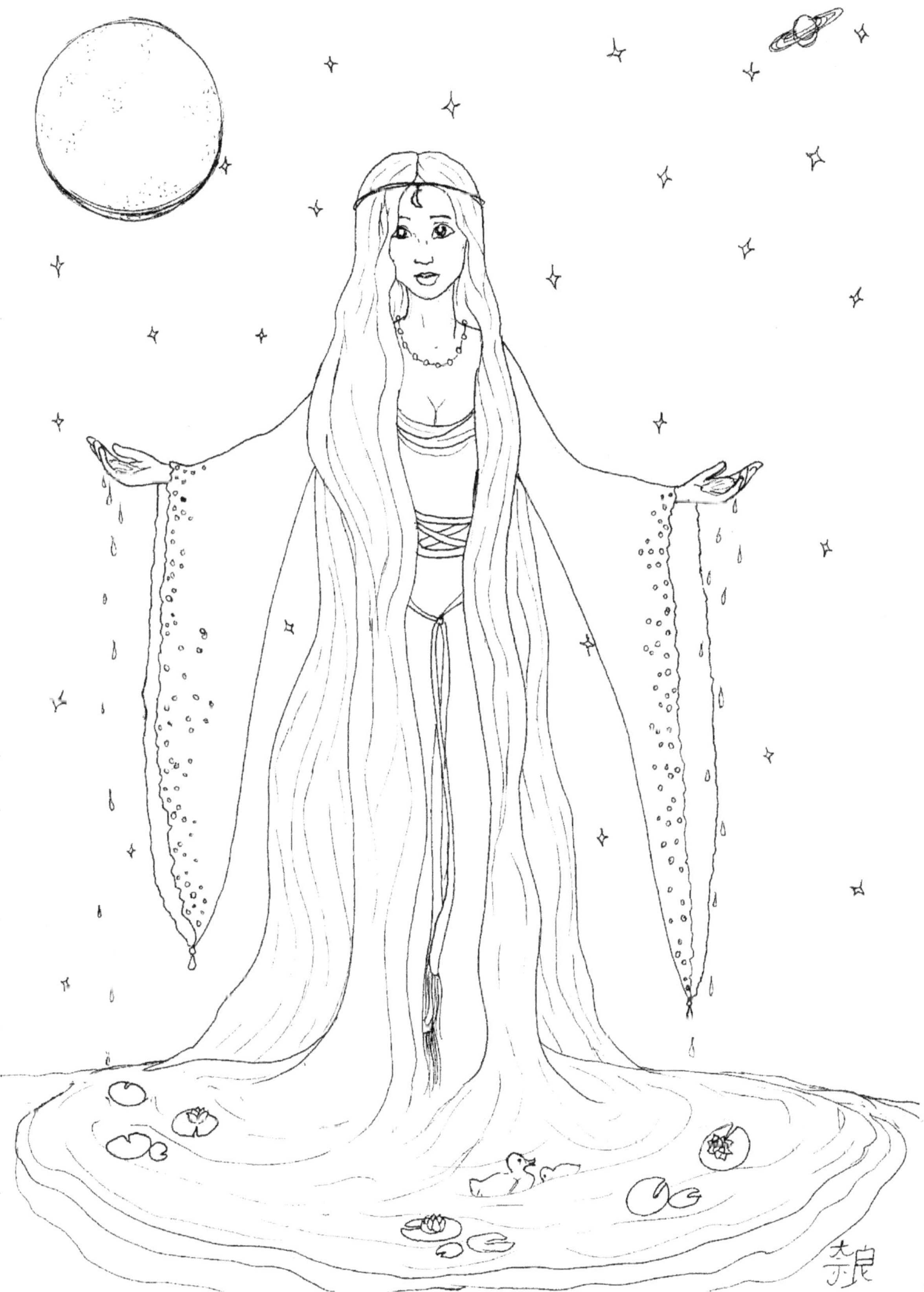

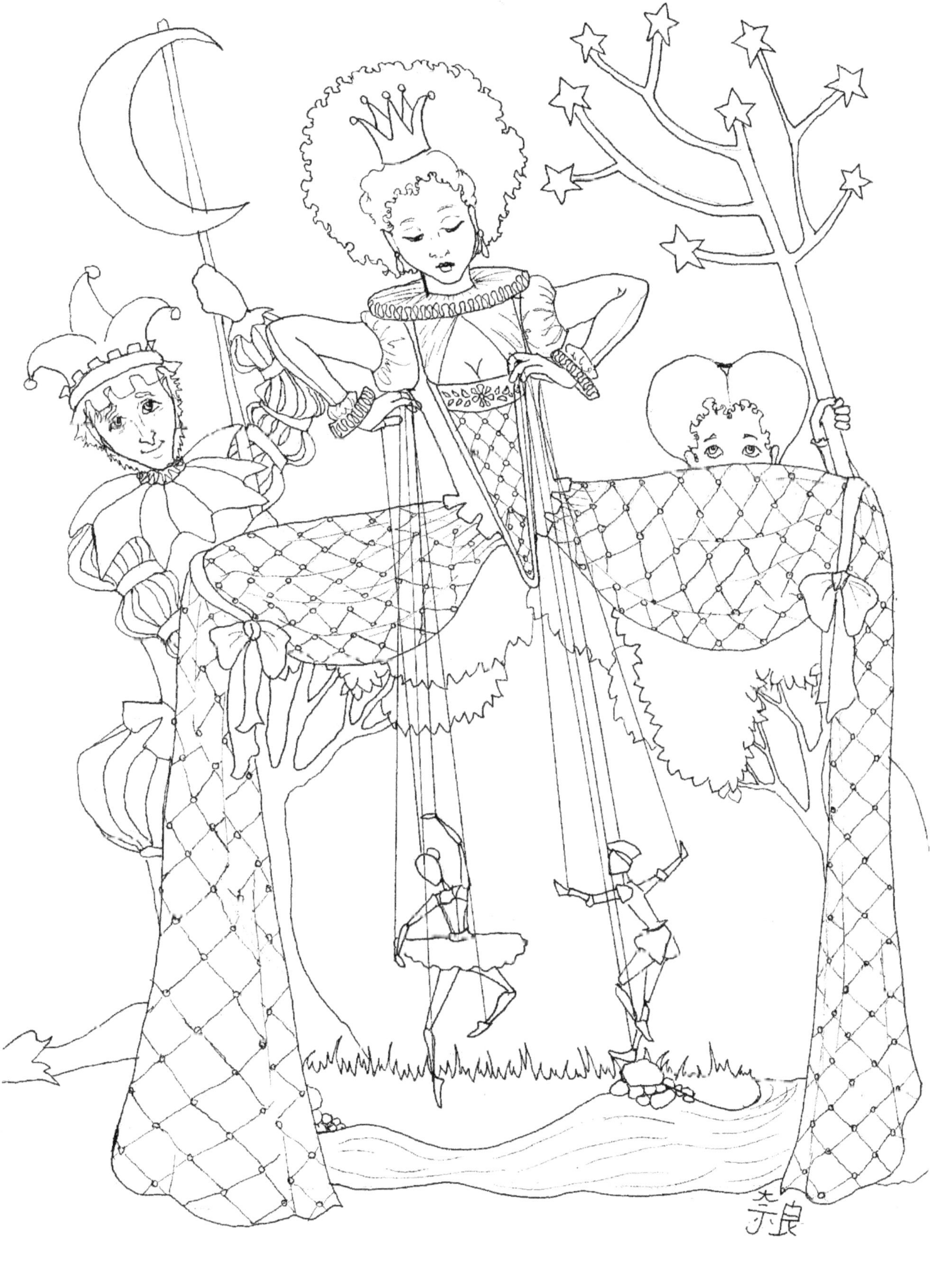
奈良

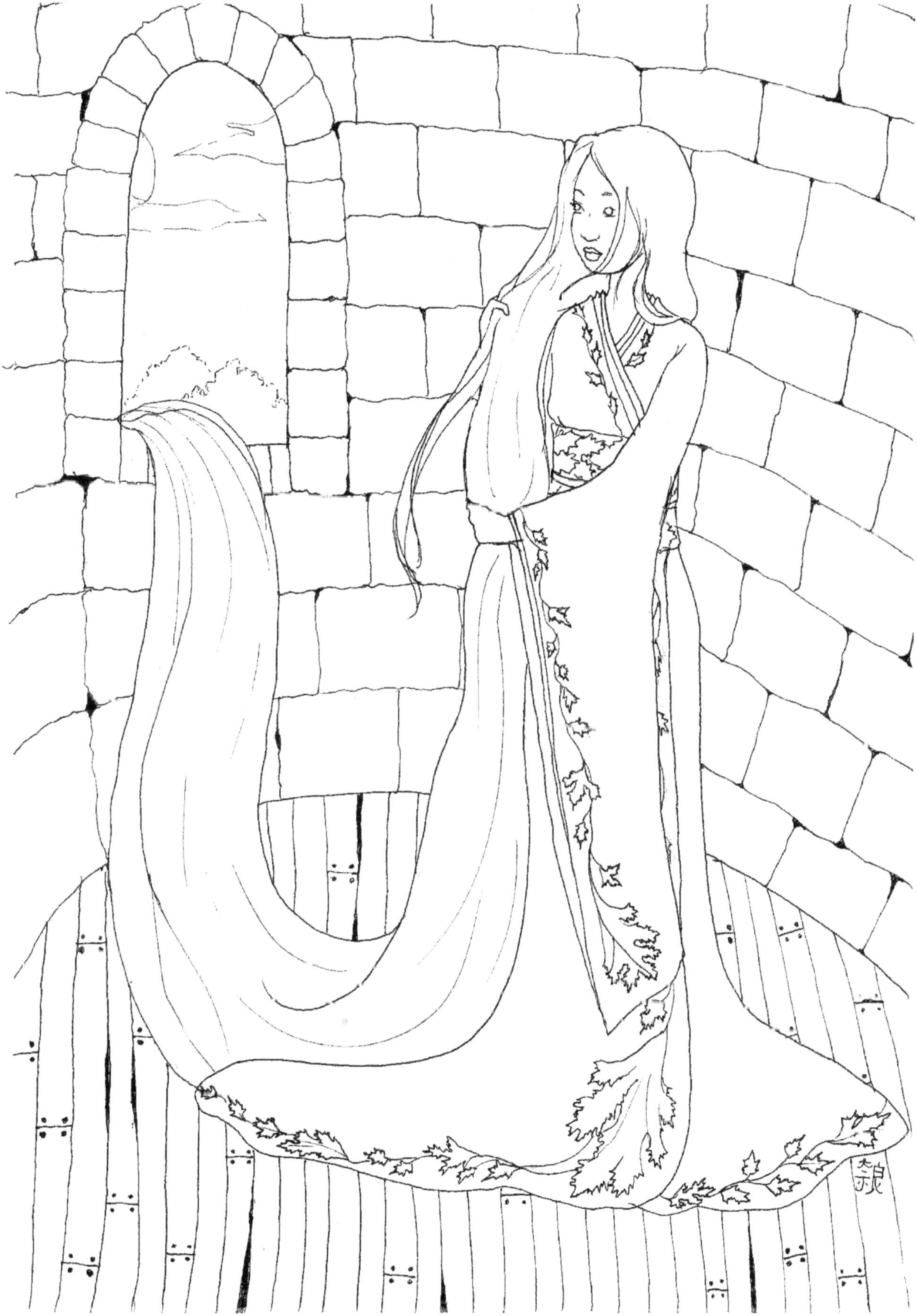

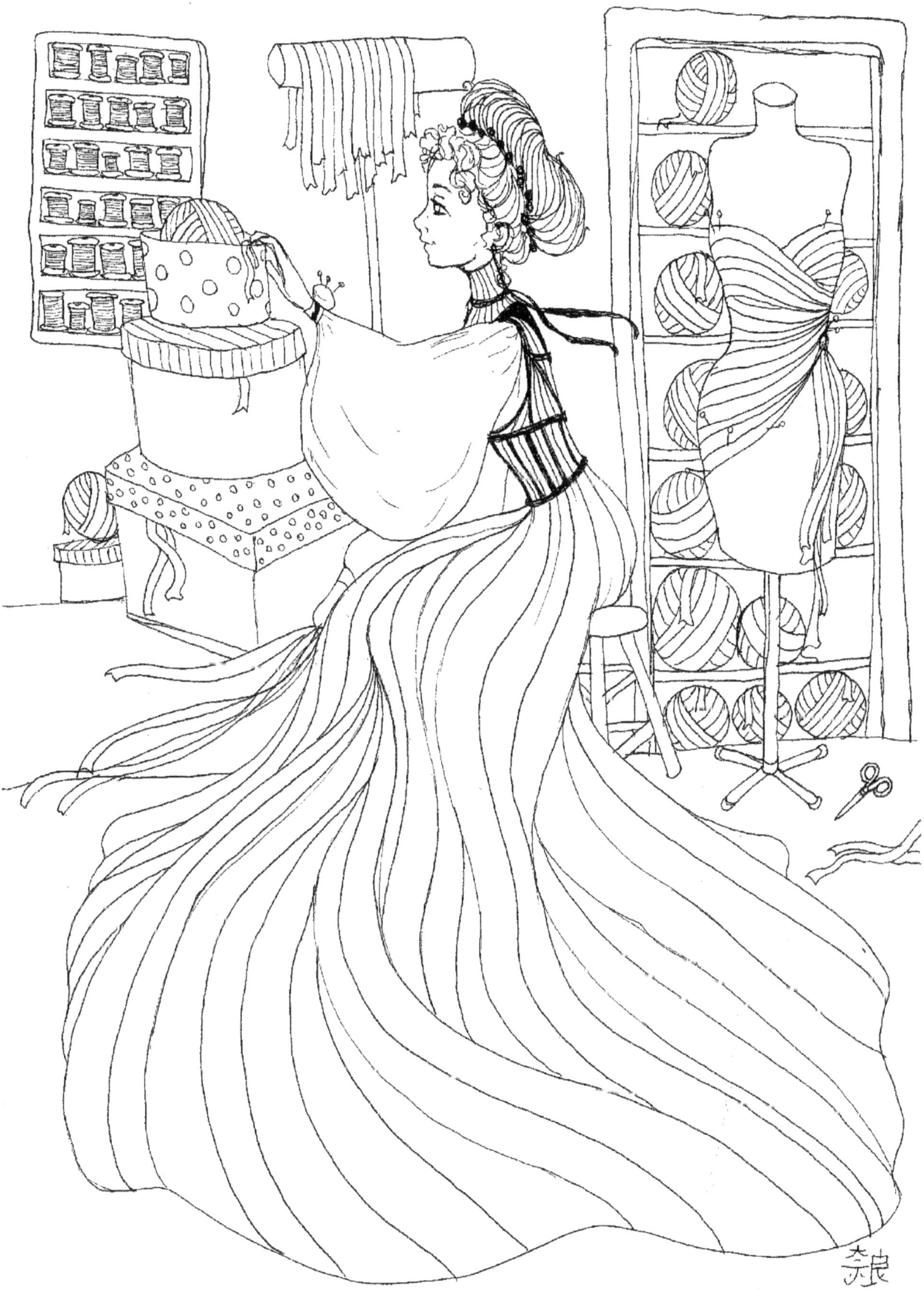

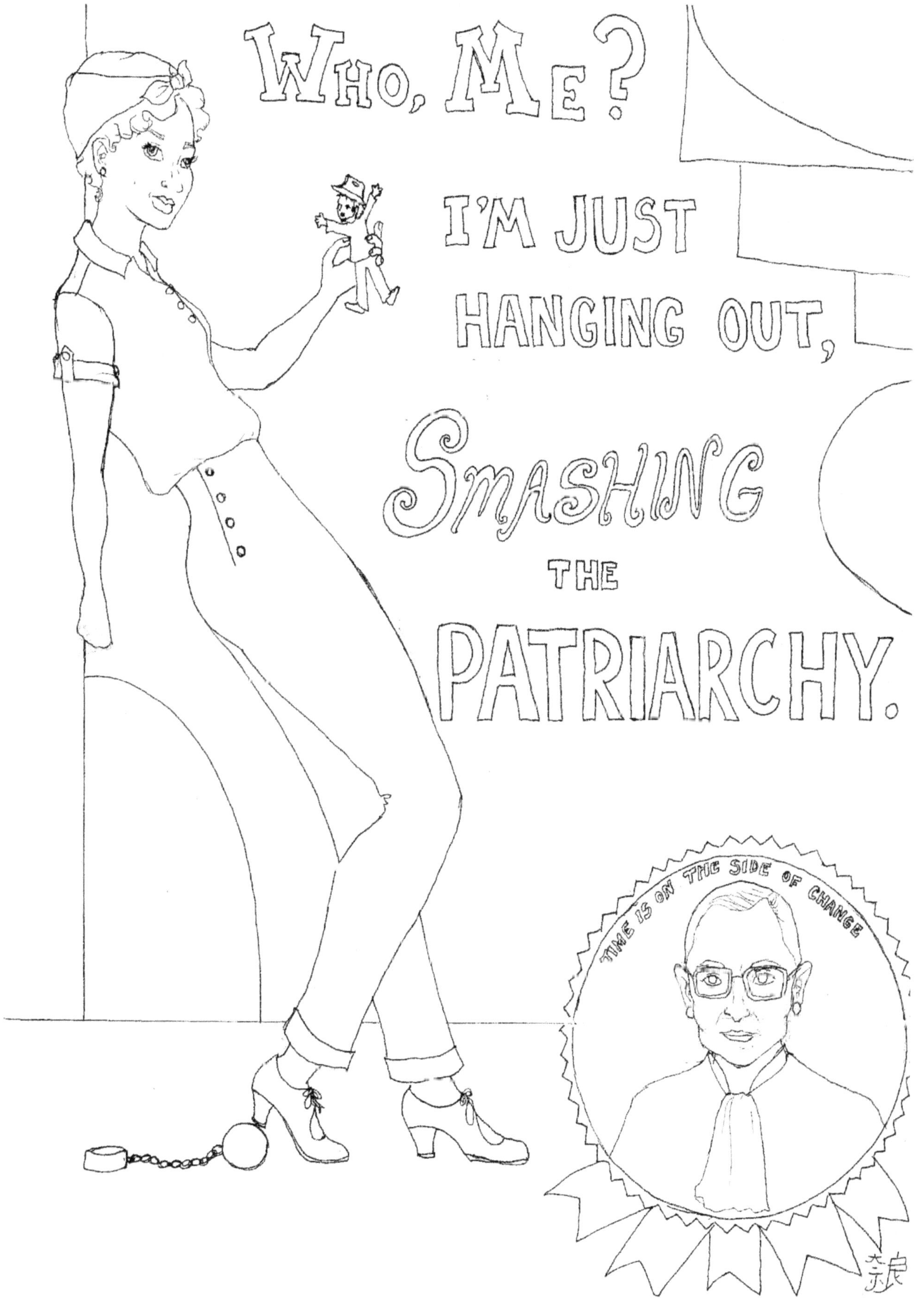
WHO, ME?
I'M JUST
HANGING OUT,
SMASHING
THE
PATRIARCHY.
TIME IS ON THE SIDE OF CHANGE

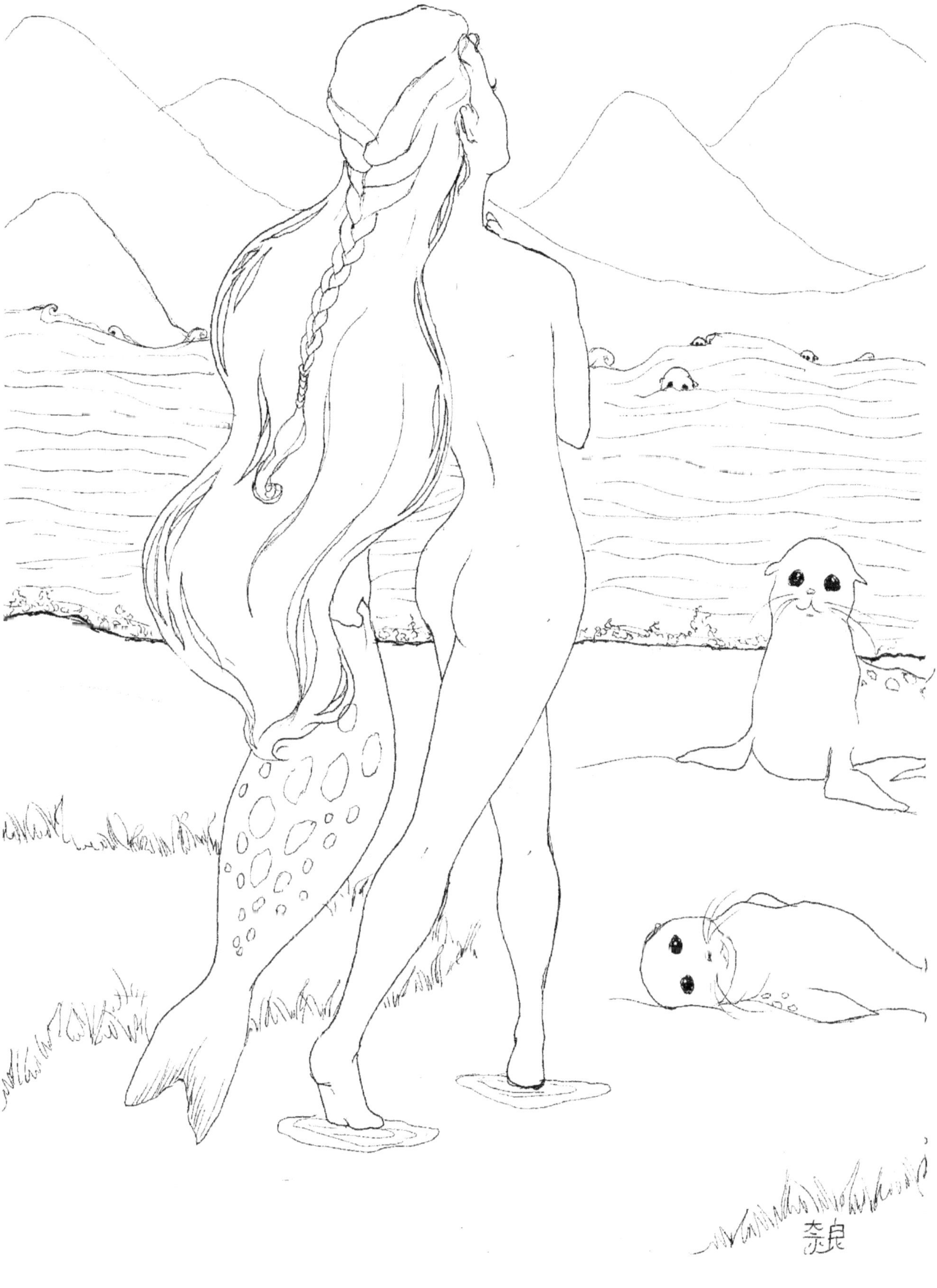
奈良

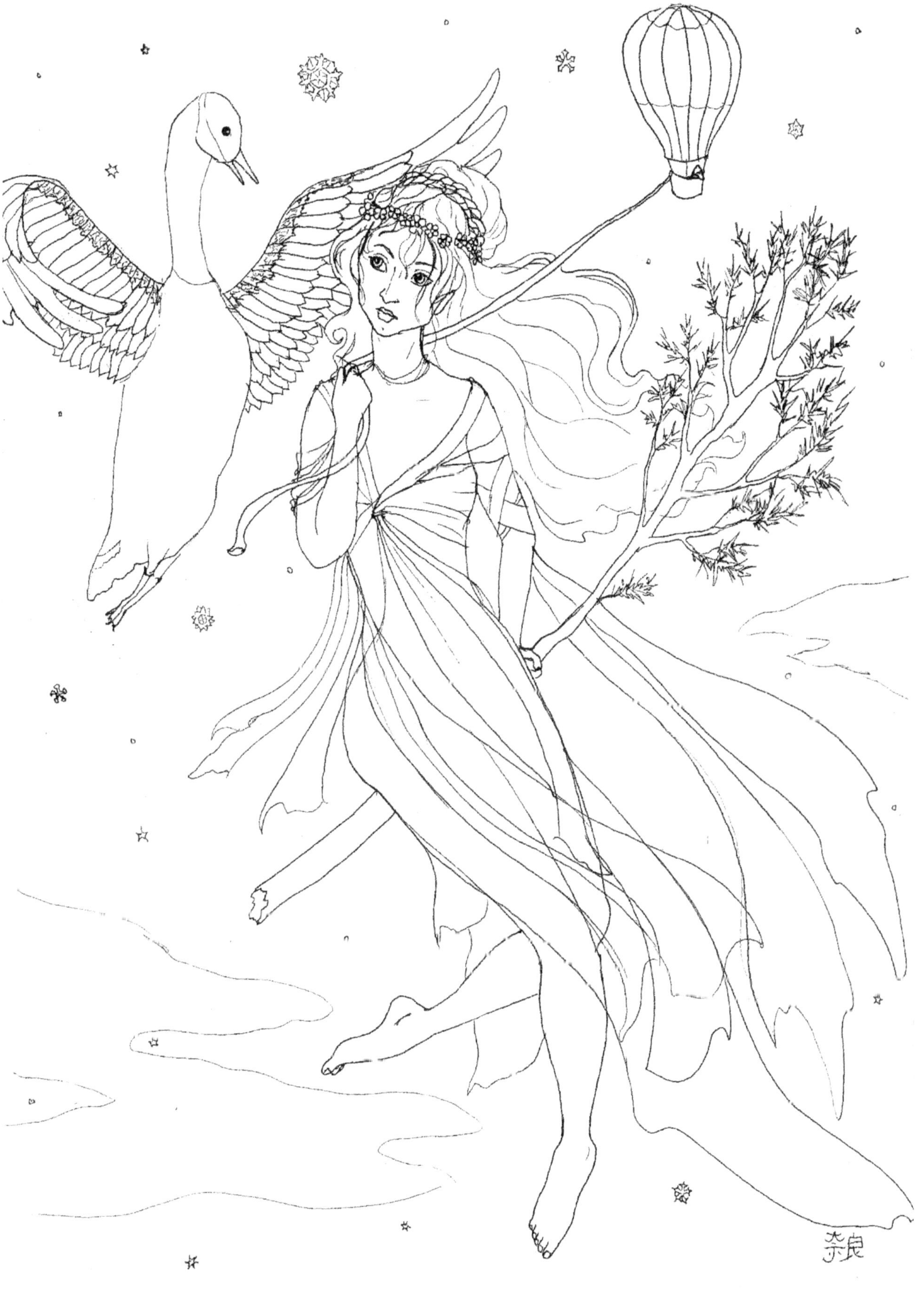

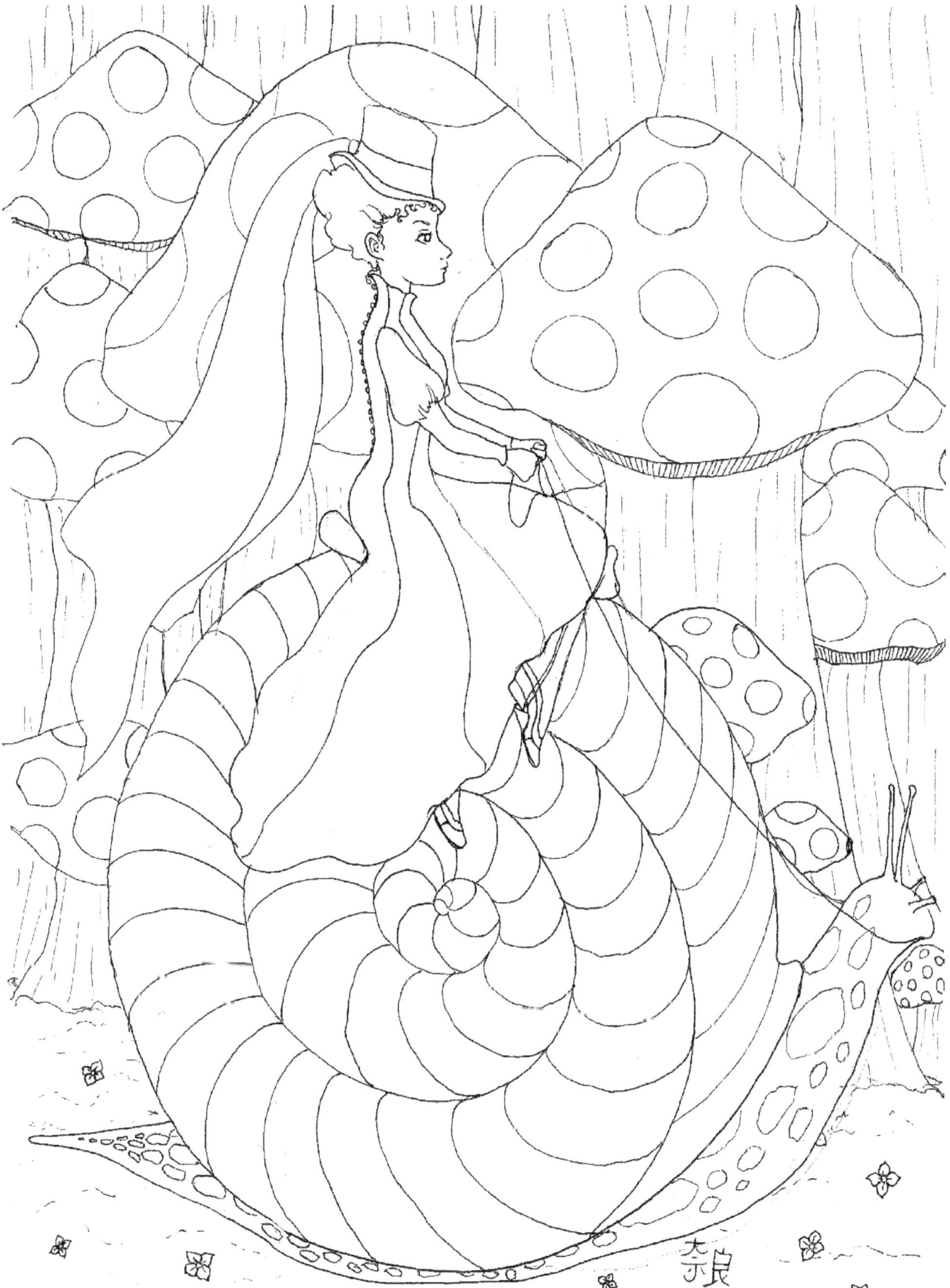
奈良

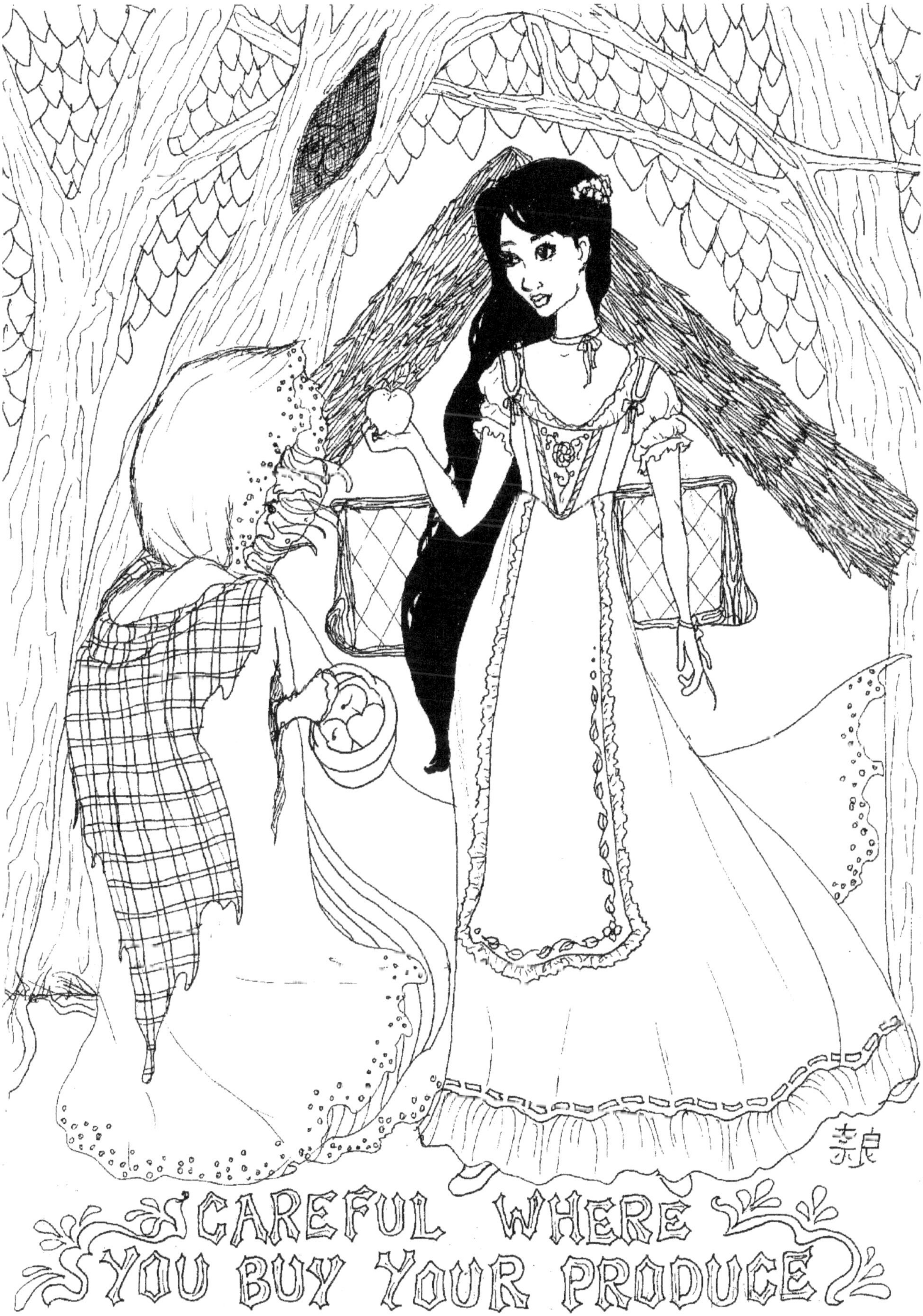
CAREFUL WHERE
YOU BUY YOUR PRODUCE

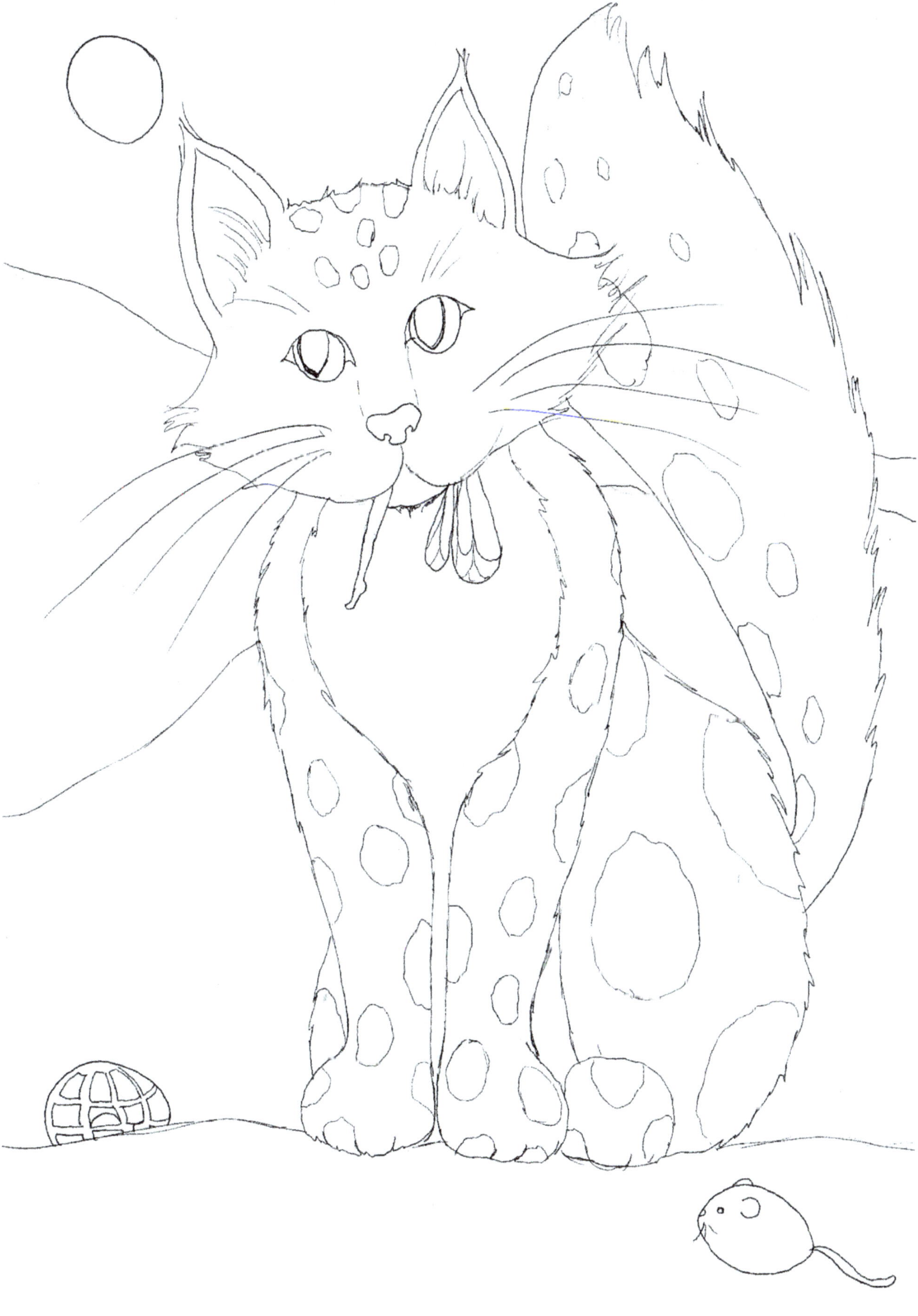

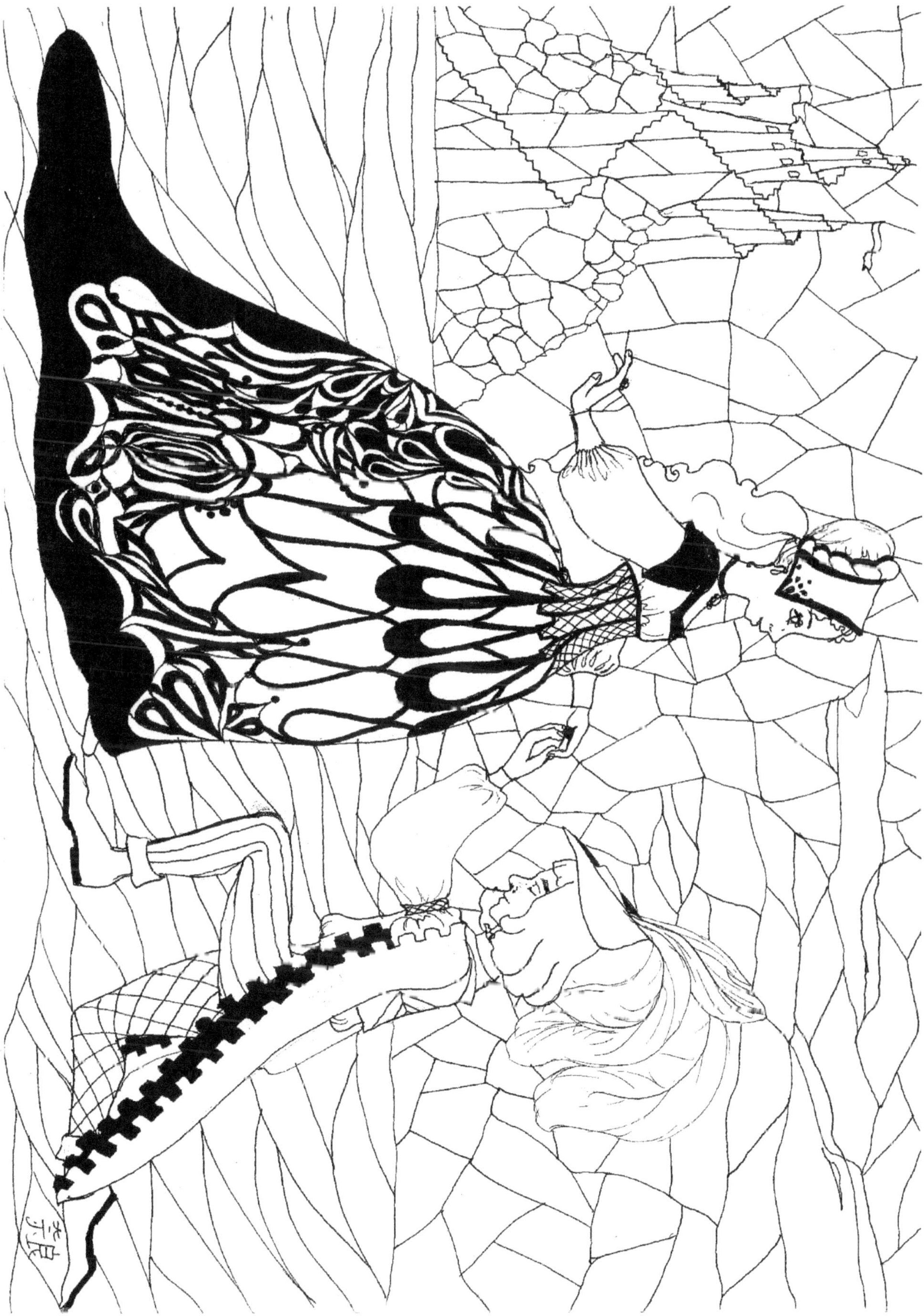

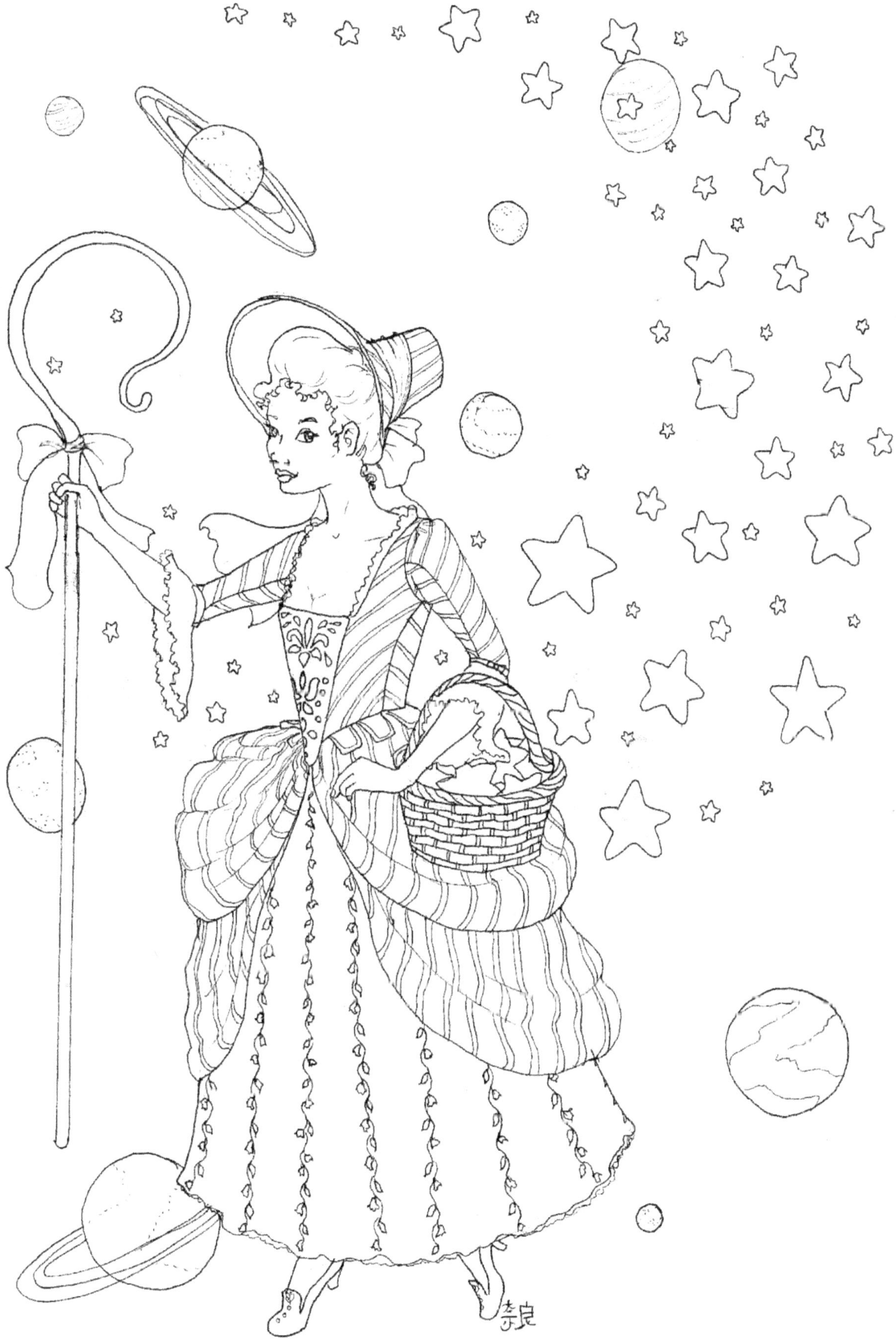

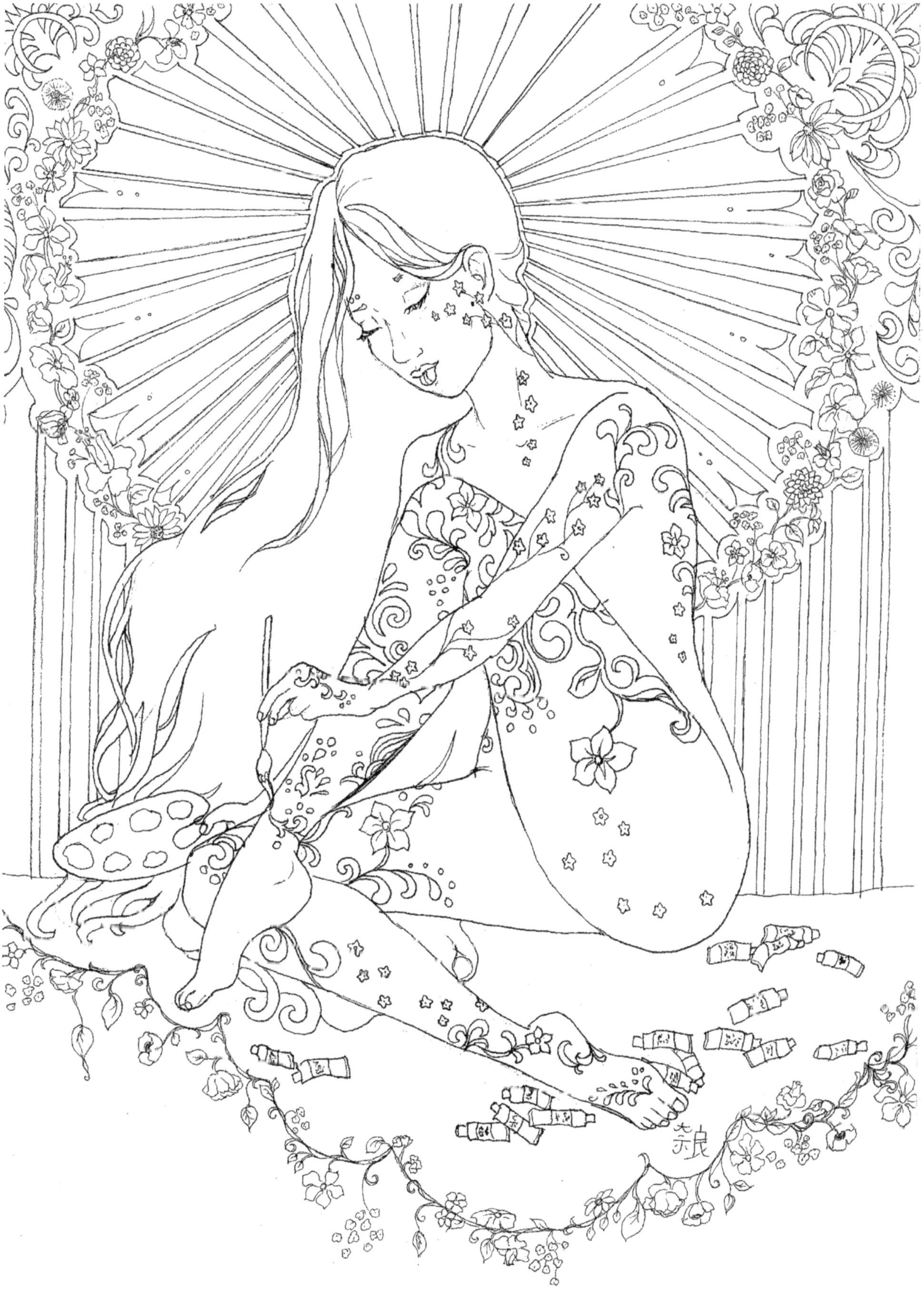
奈良

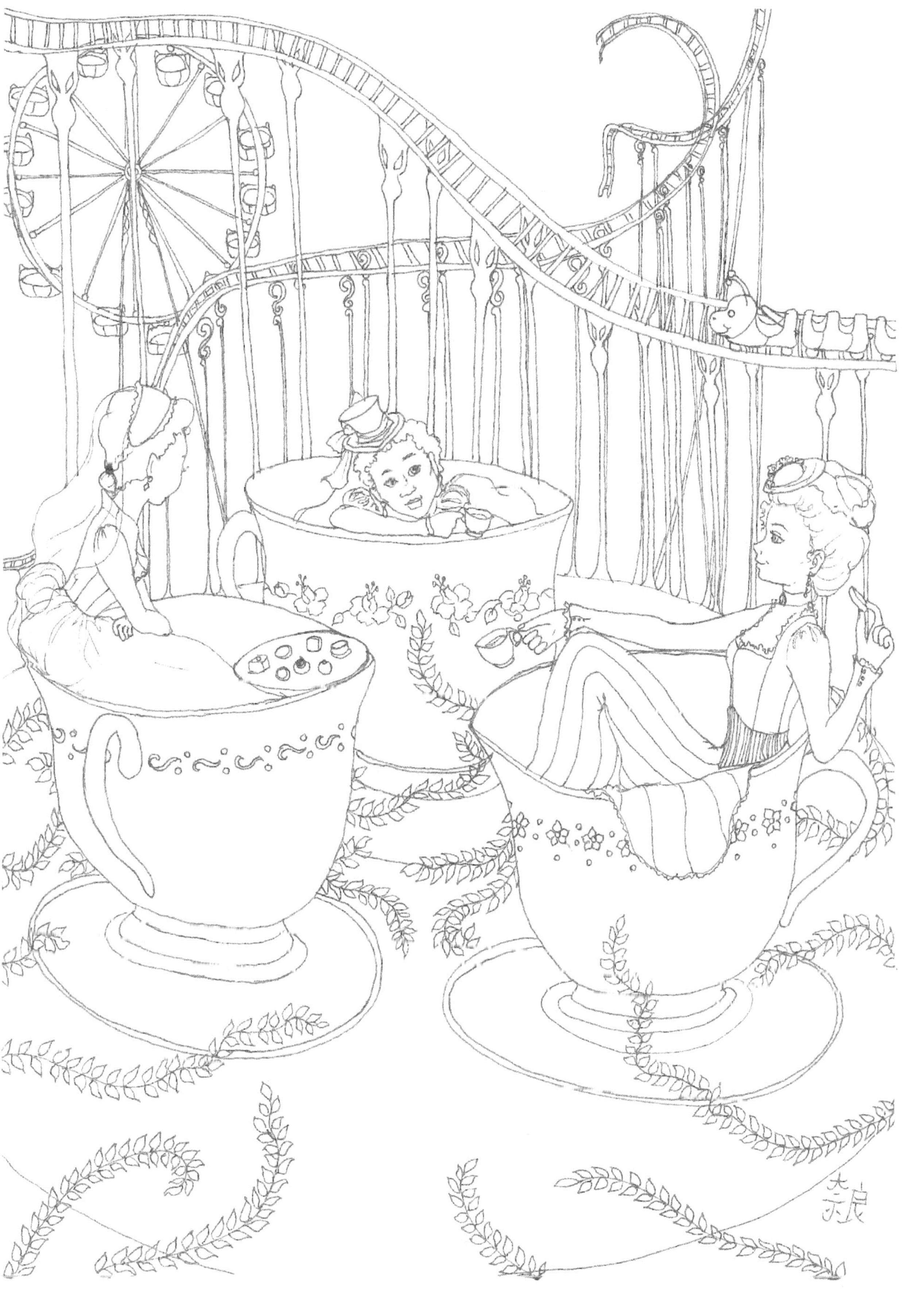

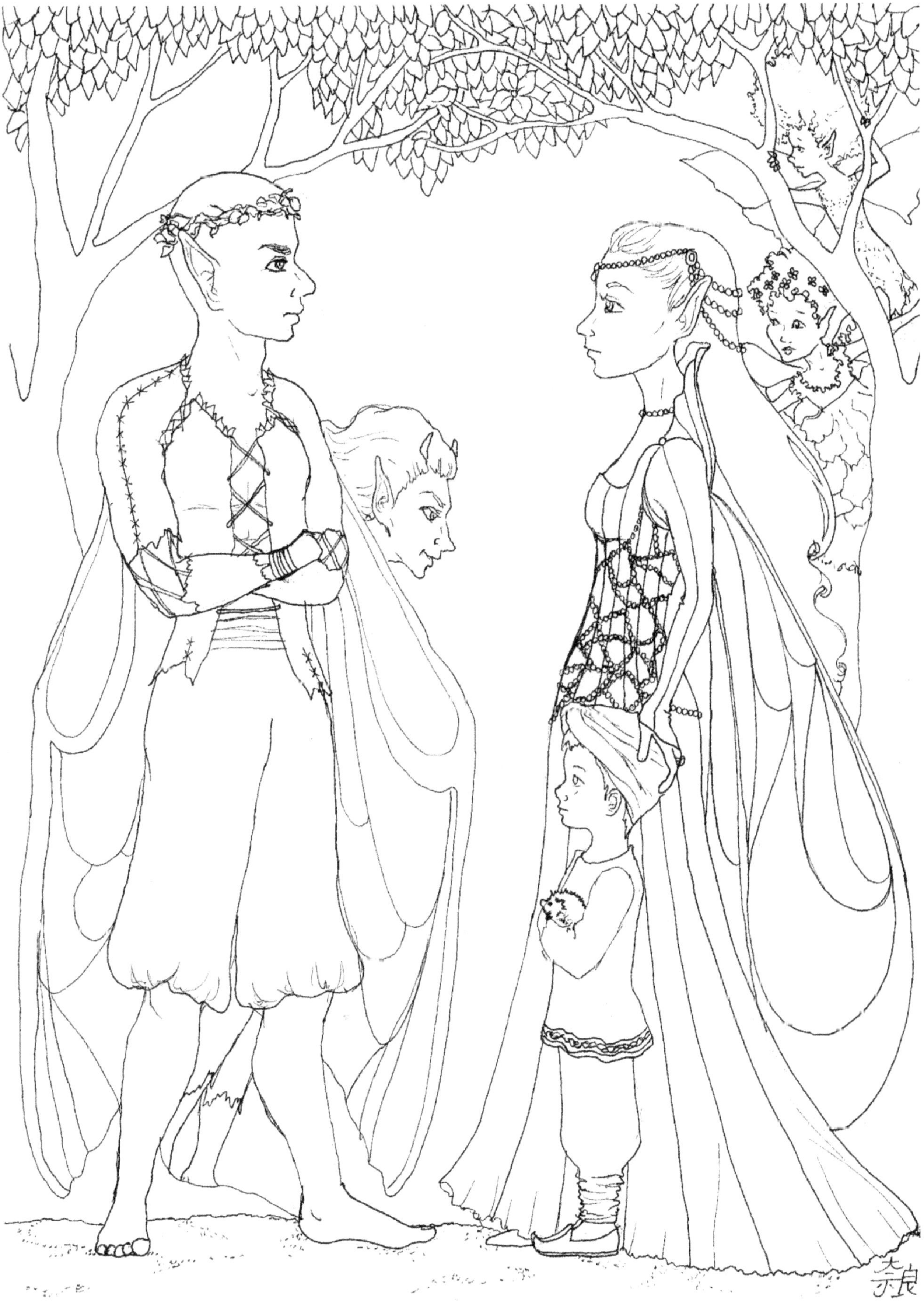

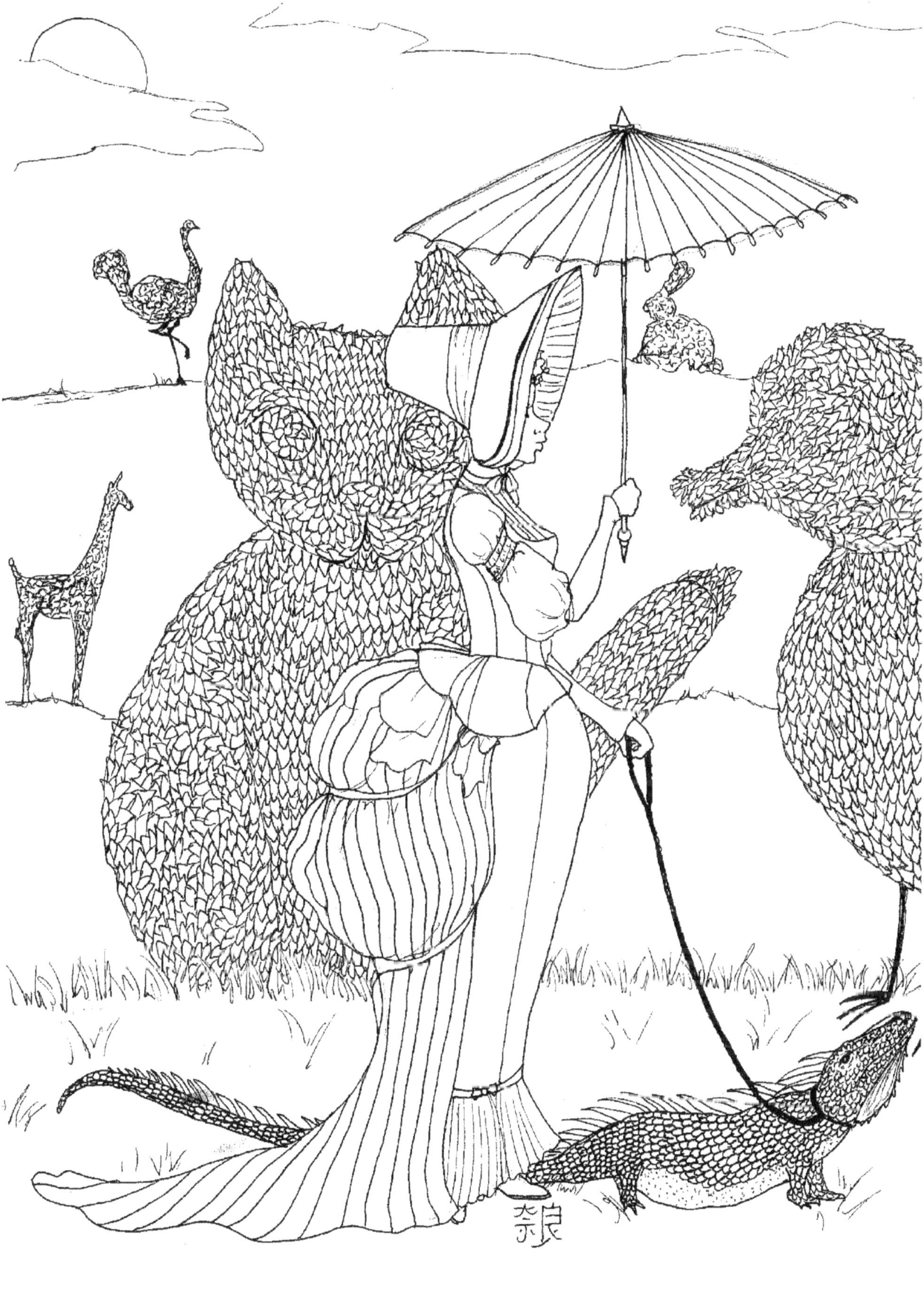

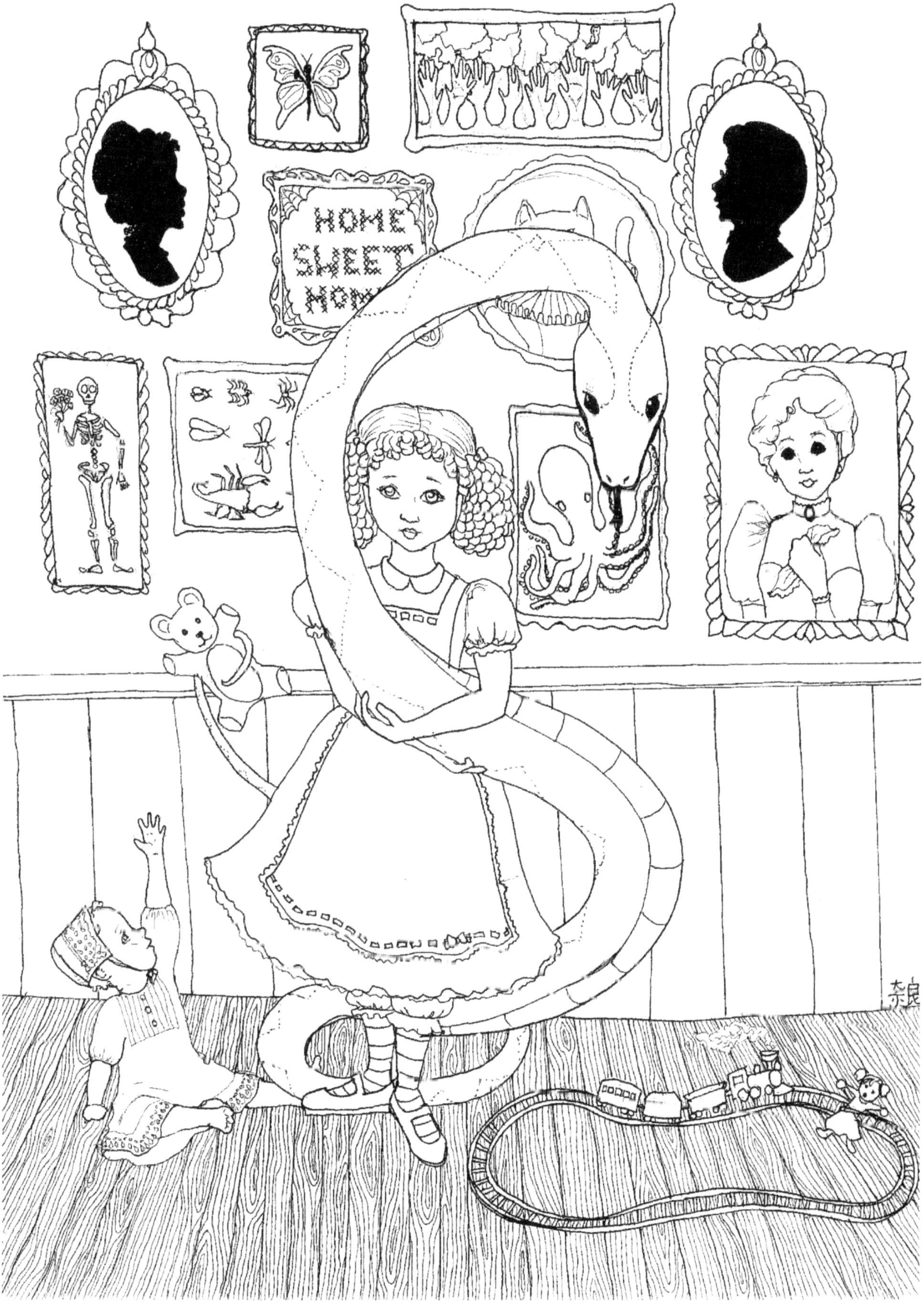
HOME
SWEET
HOM

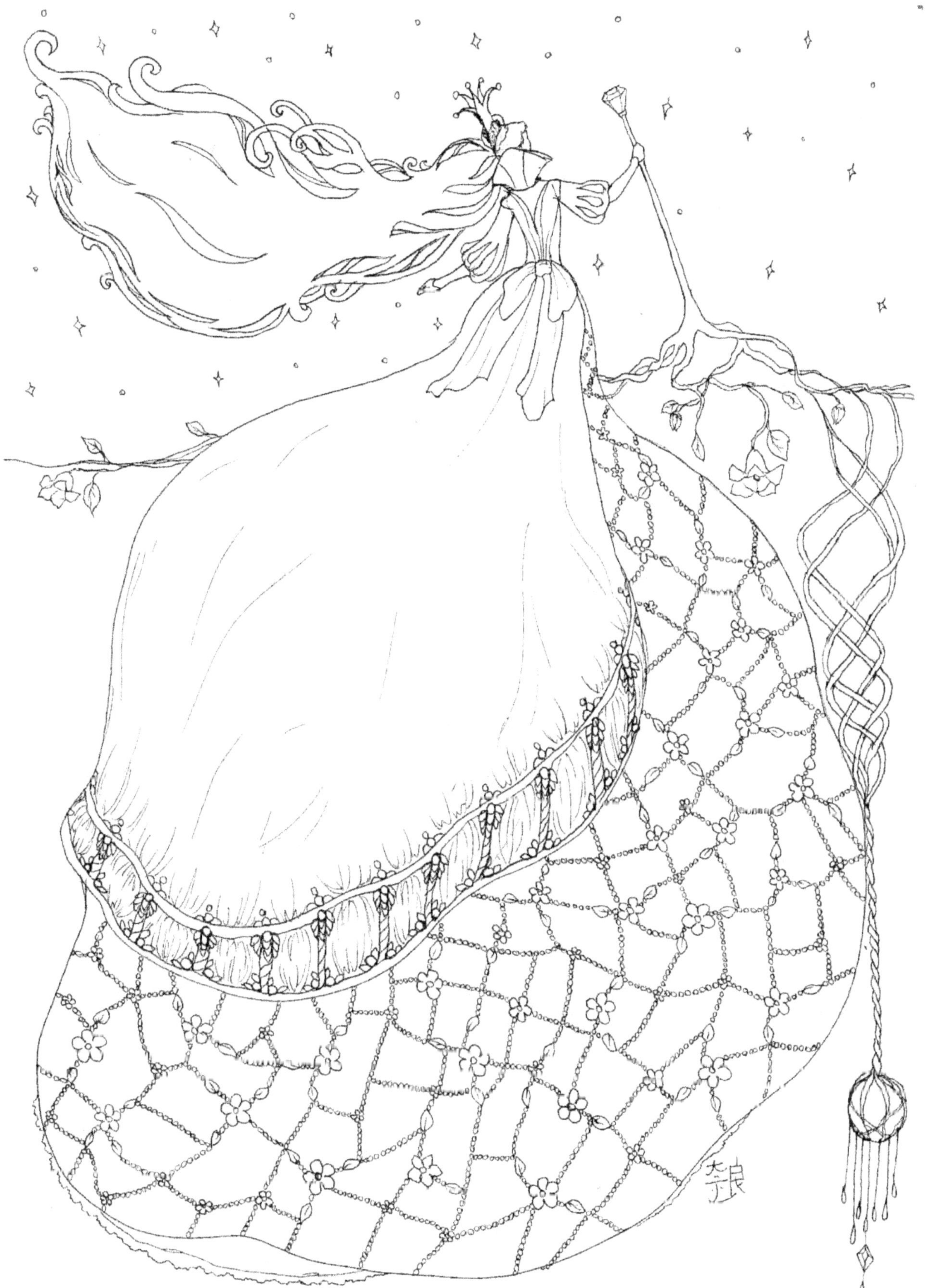